The Balkan Wars

A Captivating Guide to the First and Second Balkan War and Their Impact on World War I

Free Bonus from Captivating History
(Available for a Limited time)

Hi History Lovers!

Now you have a chance to join our exclusive history list so you can get your first history ebook for free as well as discounts and a potential to get more history books for free! Simply visit the link below to join.

Captivatinghistory.com/ebook

Also, make sure to follow us on Facebook, Twitter and Youtube by searching for Captivating History.

Contents

Introduction

The Balkan Wars, a series of conflicts that occurred between 1912 and 1913, were a complex and obscure event that shaped the history of Europe. They were, in a way, an interlude to greater events that would put all of Europe and even the whole world into a conflict. But at the time, the Balkan Wars were a product of strict nationalism, which started waking up due to the diminishing of the Ottoman Empire's power. As the Ottomans retreated from the Balkans, the people they left behind suddenly realized they belonged to an ethnic group, and they started emulating the nationalism that had previously taken hold in the Western states, such as Italy and Germany. They looked up to the West instead of their long-time oppressor, the Ottoman Empire. They strived to create large nationalist states of their own based on the model of France, Germany, and Italy. But to achieve that, these newly free people had to fight for the territory they would control.

During the First Balkan War, Bulgaria, Serbia, and Greece fought to push the Ottoman Empire even farther to the east and eventually out of Europe. They fought for the land as much as for independence. The Great Powers observed the development of the events but did not meddle until the very end. Finally, when the fighting was over, Russia, the United Kingdom, France, Germany,

Austria-Hungary, and Italy stepped in because they saw it as their duty to shape the borders in the Balkan Peninsula. Bulgaria gained the Rhodope Mountains and a large part of Western Thrace. Greece took Epirus and divided the Macedonian region with Serbia. Montenegro and Serbia divided the Sanjak of Novi Pazar, and Serbia gained Kosovo. Through the efforts of Austria-Hungary and Italy, the independent state of Albania took its shape. The Great European Powers shaped the Balkan area to fit their interests, disregarding the aspirations of the people who occupied the region. The nationalistic aspirations of these people were not satisfied.

When the fighting began in October 1912, it never really stopped in the Balkans, not even in 1914 when the whole of Europe rose to arms. The Second Balkan War was the result of the Balkan League's dissatisfaction, as they didn't agree with how the Great Powers divided the territory. Bulgaria wanted Macedonia, as it was its primary goal and the only aspiration during the First Balkan War. To be deprived of the territory for which its soldiers shed blood was unthinkable. But to acquire it, Bulgaria had to face both Serbia and Greece, two countries that stepped into an alliance to confront Bulgaria with a united front. At the time, Bulgaria had the largest army of all the Balkan League members, and it could easily defeat Serbia or Greece. But united, Serbia and Greece represented a real threat and proved a hard nut for Bulgaria to crack. The inter-allied war didn't go well for Bulgaria, and the fighting even got close to their capital of Sofia.

As if that wasn't enough, two opportunistic states, Romania and the Ottoman Empire, saw the opportunity to lay claim on parts of Bulgarian territory. Suddenly, Bulgaria had to fight four fronts, and that was impossible, even for the mightiest of the Balkan League members. The war had to stop, and this time, the Great Powers chose not to interfere but merely presented themselves as observers. That doesn't mean they didn't try to assert their influence, though to what extent is unknown. Their aspirations would be revealed later during the First World War. Many of the battlefields in this region didn't see peace until the conclusion of World War I in 1918. Even then, the Balkan states had no time to recover from the constant warfare, as only twenty years later, the region would be engulfed in the Second World War.

Chapter 1 – The Origins of the Balkan Wars

The division of territories by the Treaty of San Stefano and the Congress of Berlin
https://en.wikipedia.org/wiki/Congress_of_Berlin#/media/File:Bulgaria_San_Stefano_Berlin_1878_TB.png

The second half of the 19th century was a period when nationalistic thought started appearing in western Europe. The concept of nationalism started spreading into the Balkan Peninsula from superpowers such as Germany and France, and although its initial impact was cultural, it soon transformed into a political one. At first, the new intellectual layer of society in the Balkans worked on standardizing the vernacular languages of their countries. National art and literature started not only blooming but also spreading to those social classes that previously had no access to it.

Once the concept of nationalism seeped into the Balkans and became politicized, the people were overwhelmed with a strong desire to achieve national unity. They had to confront their Ottoman overlords and gain independence. The Balkan leaders saw no prospect in remaining a vassal to the Ottoman Empire. They thought that only through national unity could they develop national states and prosper. The Balkan leaders wanted to achieve what they saw Western powers had: political unity and economic power. They wanted to emulate Western success, and they looked up mostly to Germany as a role model of development and success. The Balkan countries adopted the Western model of nationalism and tried to use it to develop their nations. Unlike their Ottoman overlords, who divided people by religion, the Balkan people started using the concept of nationalism to achieve their geopolitical goals—the creation of separate nation-states.

In 1803, the Serbs revolted against the Ottomans, and in 1821, the Greeks did as well. The independent Greek state and the autonomous Serbian state emerged by 1830. Montenegro had gained its autonomy back in the 18th century simply because the Ottomans considered it to be remote and its people too belligerent. When the Kingdom of Italy and the German Empire attained their national unity in 1861 and 1871, respectively, they further inspired the Balkan peoples. They all envisioned the restoration of the old medieval empires on which they based their nationality. For the Bulgarians, that was the First and Second Bulgarian Empire (681–1018 and 1185–1396); for the Greeks, it was the Byzantine Empire (395–1453); and for Serbia, it was the Serbian Empire (1346–1371).

In 1876, the Montenegrins joined the Serbs in their fight against the Ottomans to establish a unified national state in the Balkans. At the same time, the Bulgarians launched their revolt against the Ottoman Empire. In 1877, Russia decided to intervene and joined the Bulgarian cause. Nine months of hard fighting ensued, but the Russians emerged from this conflict as victors. The Russo-Turkish War came to an end with the Treaty of San Stefano, which was signed in March 1878. A large and independent Bulgarian state was formed, and Serbia and Montenegro acquired even more territory at the expense of the Ottoman Empire.

The Treaty of San Stefano was extremely beneficial to Bulgaria, which achieved its dream of controlling the whole territory of the eastern Balkan Peninsula between the Danube River and the Aegean Sea. Macedonia was included in the Bulgarian state. With this, the Balkan people achieved all of their nationalistic goals.

But the Treaty of San Stefano met a negative response from the European superpowers. Germany, Great Britain, Austria-Hungary, France, Russia, and Italy thought they had a prerogative of settling all international affairs, and the Western countries wanted to limit Russian influence in the Balkans. Otto von Bismarck, the chancellor of the German Empire, offered to host a conference in which all the Great Powers would meet to settle the Balkan issue. The leading politicians of the time met in Berlin and formed a congress in 1878, which reorganized the states in the Balkans. The Bulgarian state was greatly reduced, and it lost its independence. It was transformed into an autonomous Bulgarian principality of the Ottoman Empire. Eastern Rumelia was transformed into a separate principality under Ottoman suzerainty but with a Christian ruler. Macedonia was not a part of any of the autonomous principalities; instead, it was placed under the direct control of the sultan. The Western powers disregarded Bulgarian nationalism and brought back Ottoman rule to counter the Russian presence in the Balkan Peninsula.

The Congress of Berlin recognized the independence of Serbia, but Montenegro had to give up its claims on territories in Herzegovina, the Sanjak of Novi Pazar, and northern Albania. Austria-Hungary then proceeded to occupy Bosnia, Herzegovina, and the Sanjak of Novi Pazar. Although these territories were under occupation, they remained under the de jure control of the Ottoman Empire.

However, the Montenegrins and Serbs continued their aspirations to gain these territories for themselves. Romania gained independence, but it had to give up on Bessarabia, which was given to Russia. Instead, Romania received Northern Dobruja on the Bulgarian border. The Congress of Berlin failed to resolve the tension between Greece and the Ottoman Empire, and this finally culminated in 1881 when Greece annexed Thessaly and some territories in southern Epirus. The Great Powers simply sanctioned these Greek gains.

No one was really satisfied with the results of the Congress of Berlin. Russia was disappointed that, as the winner of the Russo-Turkish War, it received almost no prize. Bulgaria was reduced to a small portion of what its nationalists had envisioned before the endeavors to expel the Ottomans out of the Balkans, and it lost its independence. They felt betrayed and crippled. The Bulgarian leaders continued to strive for a larger Bulgaria, and they were not alone in their frustration. The Greeks, Serbs, and Montenegrins felt that the Treaty of Berlin, which replaced the Treaty of San Stefano, limited their national aspirations. They all felt the need to overcome the Congress of Berlin and fight for their national independence and unity.

National Aspirations

In 1885, Bulgaria acted against the Treaty of Berlin. They unilaterally proclaimed unification with Eastern Rumelia, relying on the fact that, up until now, the Great Powers had not done anything to preserve the settlement reached during the Congress of Berlin. But later that year, Serbia allied with Austria-Hungary and attacked Bulgaria. The Bulgarians managed to defeat Serbia and preserve their unification.

Although Serbia admitted defeat, Bulgaria planned an invasion that would have probably occurred if the Austro-Hungarian Empire didn't intervene. The animosity between the two Balkan states was so great that the hopes of a unified Balkan Peninsula against the Ottoman Empire failed. Due to the dynastic rivalries, Serbia and Montenegro never reached national unity as they initially intended. The internal division between the Balkan states prevented them from mounting a unified effort against their Ottoman overlords.

However, these states had tried to make efforts in the past to be more united. Around twenty years prior to Serbia's attack on Bulgaria, the idea of a Balkan alliance was conceived. The Serbian leaders decided to assist the Bulgarian revolutionists and shelter them.

So, relying on the fact that Serbia and Bulgaria had worked together in the past, the Greek prime minister, Charilaos Trikoupis, proposed an alliance between Serbia, Greece, and Bulgaria in 1891. The Slavic states weren't enthusiastic about such an alliance because they had no interests in the Aegean region and because all three states wanted to claim Macedonia. However, by 1897, Serbia and Bulgaria had finally decided they could work jointly in Macedonia.

Disappointed by the failure to establish an alliance with Bulgaria and Serbia, Greece decided to claim Crete. The war between Greece and Turkey lasted for only thirty days. The Ottomans had no trouble defending their territory from Greek attacks, but once they showed an interest in claiming Greek territory, the Great Powers reacted to preserve the Berlin settlement. They sent their troops to Crete to stop the Greeks from retaliating against the island's Muslim population. The result was the autonomy of Crete, which was shielded by a commission founded by the Great Powers. Any idea of unification with Greece was destroyed. The failure of Greece to annex Crete showed other Balkan states that they would never be able to defeat the Ottomans alone, even though the empire's power was slowly fading.

The Bulgarians wanted Thrace, the Greeks wanted the Aegean Islands, and Serbia wanted Bosnia and Herzegovina. And all three states had an interest in Macedonia. Only the Montenegrins remained uninterested in that territory since they were cut off from it. But they had their eye on the part of the territory that is today northern Albania (then the Ottoman Empire).

The Ottoman rule made Macedonia the center of the Balkan Peninsula, but Macedonia was a territory that shared Serbian, Bulgarian, and Greek cultural and linguistic heritages since early medieval times. Those who inhabited this territory had a different idea than the outside states. In 1893, the Macedonians created the Internal Macedonian Revolutionary Organization (IMRO), whose slogan was "Macedonia for the Macedonians." They wanted independence, but at times, they even defended the idea of an autonomous Macedonian state within the Ottoman Empire rather than annexation by any of the Balkan states.

To counter the IMRO and to acquire Thrace, the Bulgarian government established the Supreme Macedonian-Adrianople Committee in 1895, which was a political organization that promoted revolutionary ideas with the goal of eventual annexation of Macedonia and Thrace. In 1894, Greece founded the Ethniki Etaireia, a nationalistic organization with the goal of liberating all Greek people that were still under Ottoman rule, which would include Macedonia. Before that, in 1886, Serbia made the Society of Saint Sava, a non-governmental organization that offered protection to all Serbs living in Ottoman territories as well as in Austria-Hungary. All of these organizations used propaganda as their main tool of operation, but they also served to gather paramilitary minds. In response, the Ottoman government sent arms to organizations that promoted Islamic opportunities to various ethnicities within the empire.

There was another territorial unity that was a thorn in the eye of the Balkan states, mainly Serbia and Montenegro. That was the Sanjak of Novi Pazar, which is today Kosovo. Both Serbian states laid claim to it, even though the population of Sanjak was a hodgepodge of Serbs, Albanians, Vlachs, the Romani people, Turks, and Slavic-speaking Muslims. The majority of the population was Serbian, and they regarded the efforts of the Serbian Army as liberation. Serbia and Montenegro called this territory "Old Serbia" because it used to be the core of the Serbian Empire. It was also the place where the famous Battle of Kosovo took place in 1389, which was when the Balkan forces under Serbian leadership fought the invading Ottomans. The rivalry over Macedonia and the Sanjak of Novi Pazar would escalate significantly at the end of the 19th century.

In 1903, a pro-Austro-Hungarian king, Alexander Obrenovic, was murdered in Serbia in a conspiracy to put the nationalist Karadjordjevic dynasty on the throne. Petar Karadjordjevic was anti-Habsburg, which was the dynasty that ruled Austria-Hungary. In 1904, Peter made an alliance with the Bulgarian nationalists to promote each other's economy and provide mutual military assistance. They also made an agreement of mutual action in Macedonia and Kosovo. But this alliance achieved nothing because the relations between Bulgaria and Serbia worsened due to Habsburg pressure. Serbia then offered an alliance to Montenegro, but since these countries experienced rivalries over who would be the leader of the Serbs' nationalistic movement, the alliance was never realized.

When Russia suffered a revolution in 1905, in which the Romanov royal family agreed to transfer power to a constitutional monarchy, the Balkan states realized they could no longer count on outside military help. The Russians were no longer able to promote and preserve the

Bulgarian state they had created with the Treaty of San Stefano. The Bulgarian leaders finally realized they had to strengthen their army if they wanted to wage war against the Ottomans and liberate themselves.

Crisis in Bosnia

In 1908, a group of officers in the Ottoman army named the Committee of Unity and Progress usurped the empire and announced a series of reforms that would ensure progress. They were led by Enver Pasha, and the group became better known as the Young Turks. Besides wanting to ensure the progress and modernization of the Ottoman Empire, the Young Turks wanted to stop its disintegration by creating an Ottoman identity among the many nations who lived within the empire. To modernize their army, the Young Turks invited German and British generals to help them initiate the process. When a counter-revolt was mounted in 1909, the Young Turks exiled the old sultan, Abdul Hamid II, and replaced him with the younger and more compliant Mehmed V.

Austria and Russia needed to counter the Ottoman influence in the Balkans because they had their own goals in the area. Austria wanted to annex Bosnia and Herzegovina, and Russia wanted to control the strait that linked the Black Sea and the Aegean Sea. This was crucial to control the trade between Europe and Asia, as well as the movement of armies. Because of this, Austria and Russia agreed to support each other in the Balkans.

The Great Powers sanctioned Russia's plan to take control of the strait, but Austria disagreed. In turn, Russia demanded that Austria abandon its plans for the annexation of Bosnia, but no one reacted. The Austrians did retreat from their garrison in the Sanjak of Novi Pazar, but nothing more. Russia suffered a diplomatic defeat and had to find the means to restore its power and influence in the Balkans.

Other Balkan states became concerned with the Ottoman nationhood that the Young Turks wanted to promote throughout their empire because they believed that would undermine their nationalistic plans. When Austria-Hungary finally annexed Bosnia later in 1908, the result was the agitation of the whole Balkan Peninsula, as both Serbs and Montenegrins believed they had suffered a great blow to their nationalistic aspirations. Aware of their weakness and isolation, Serbia and Montenegro finally reached an agreement and formed an alliance directed against the Habsburgs. They also agreed to establish a mutual border in the territory of the Sanjak of Novi Pazar, which was still a part of the Ottoman Empire that separated Serbia and Montenegro, although it was occupied by Austria-Hungary. The Habsburgs abandoned Sanjak in 1909, but the Serbian-Montenegrin alliance didn't last long enough to call this a victory. Instead, the alliance was disassembled by the old nationalistic rivalries between the two states.

The Bulgarians were the only Balkan people to get something out of the Bosnian crisis. They used its annexation as a cover to declare independence from the Ottomans, and their prince Ferdinand proclaimed himself as the tsar. To them, the annexation of Bosnia represented a degradation of the Treaty of Berlin, which was the only legal obstacle the Balkan states had to realize their national aspirations. The political current had changed, and the actions of Austria-Hungary, as well as the lack of reaction from the Great Powers, showed that everyone wished to get rid of the Treaty of Berlin.

Greek officers rebelled in 1909, and like the Young Turks, they overthrew the government. The new Greek government wanted to take advantage of the Balkan crisis, and they pushed an overtly nationalistic policy. The previous year, when Austria-Hungary annexed Bosnia and when Bulgaria declared independence, Crete announced it had joined Greece. But the new Greek government was unable to put this union in effect. The Great Powers remained indifferent, allowing the Ottomans to interfere in Crete's union with Greece. The tensions between them heightened the next year when the Great Powers withdrew the commission that had controlled the situation in Crete since 1898. War was imminent, but it was averted because Greek Prime Minister Eleftherios Venizelos (also spelled as Eleutherios Venizelos) refused to give parliamentary seats to representatives from Crete.

Albanian Awakening

The Albanians had supported the Ottoman rule of the Balkan Peninsula since its beginnings in the medieval period. They shared the Islamic faith and culture with the Turks, and because of that, they were given special privileges from Constantinople. They were allowed to possess weapons and paid reduced taxes. Albanians came to represent a majority of the population in Ottoman-controlled regions of Ioannina, the Vilayet of Manastir, and Scutari. Albanians of these regions supported the Young Turks and their government in Constantinople. They believed the reforms the Young Turks instigated in the Ottoman Empire would eventually lead to the recognition of Albanian autonomy. But these hopes weren't based on anything the Young Turks had to offer, and the Albanians ended up disappointed.

In fact, the new Ottoman government strived to centralize the empire. The Albanians suddenly faced the loss of their privileges and assimilation. The first to revolt were the Catholic Albanian tribes in the northern provinces in the winter of 1910. The next year, other Albanian tribes joined the revolt. They founded the Albanian Committee in Vlore and demanded the unification of Ioannina, Scutari, Manastir, and Kosovo into an autonomous Albanian province. Although Mehmed V agreed to open talks with the Albanians and even visited Kosovo to show his goodwill, the issue wasn't resolved before the outbreak of the First Balkan War.

The Albanian aspirations to take Kosovo challenged those of Serbia and Montenegro. These Slavic nations believed that Austria-Hungary was behind the awakening of Albanian national self-awareness, and they knew they had to act quickly. Montenegrins also hoped they would claim parts of what is today northern Albania, including the important city of Scutari. If the Albanians were to achieve their autonomy, these territories would be lost forever. The Greeks were also concerned about the Albanian awakening because they claimed parts of Epirus. Greece also didn't want to get involved in a war with the Ottoman Empire too soon, as their army wasn't ready. The Albanian national awakening threatened Serbia, Montenegro, and Greece, so these three states finally chose to act together.

Chapter 2 – The Balkan League

A military poster from 1912 promoting the Balkan League. A Bulgarian, Serb, Montenegrin, and Greek are seen in their national garments, shaking hands. In the background is Hagia Sophia, represented as an Orthodox church.
https://en.wikipedia.org/wiki/Balkan_League#/media/File:Balkan_Lea gue_and_Hagia_Sophia.jpg

The Foundation of the League

After the annexation of Bosnia, Austro-Hungarian policies became extremely anti-Serbian. Because of this, Serbia sought to strengthen its relations with other Balkan nations, and it reached out to Bulgaria in an effort to resolve their national unity issues. The two countries were aware they had to act before the Young Turks fully implemented their reforms and achieved the notion of Ottoman identity.

Another reason for the alliance between Bulgaria and Serbia was the radicalization they experienced among their internal organizations. The Internal Macedonian Revolutionary Organization (IMRO) failed in the Macedonian uprising, but it started operating in Bulgaria and was out of the government's control. In Serbia, the secret military society known as the Black Hand functioned outside of Belgrade's reach. The trouble became even greater when some government officials started sympathizing with the Black Hand. Both Bulgarian and Serbian organizations decided to work on national unity without governmental approval and disregarded the government's sanctions. Sofia and Belgrade realized that if they wanted to keep their national movements under control, they had to act quickly against the Ottoman Empire.

However, to be able to unite against the Ottomans, the Balkan nations first had to overcome the issues they had between themselves. Russia took advantage of the willingness the Balkan states were expressing in working together and started pushing its Balkan interests forward. The Russians started encouraging the formation of an anti-Austrian bloc in the Balkans, and the Russian ambassadors stationed in Belgrade and Sofia started working on bringing Serbia and Bulgaria together.

In 1911, they decided to finally address the Macedonian issue. The Bulgarian prime minister, Ivan Evstratiev Geshov, was convinced that the national aspirations of his country would never attain "the Bulgaria" that was envisioned by the Treaty of San Stefano. And if it was in an alliance with Serbia, they could seize a significant portion of Macedonia.

Later that year, the Italo-Turkish War started, providing an incentive for the Balkan nations to hurry up and reach an agreement. This war further undermined the Treaty of Berlin and weakened the Ottoman Empire's army, which only benefited the Balkan states. The alliance negotiations started between Prime Minister Geshov and his Serbian counterpart, Milovan Milovanovic, and they lasted for three months. Russia provided them with diplomatic assistance, and the agreement was finally signed on March 7th, 1912.

The agreement formed an alliance between Serbia and Bulgaria against both the Ottoman and Habsburg Empires, and it also decided the fate of Macedonia. If autonomy for Macedonia couldn't be gained, Bulgaria and Serbia agreed to divide the territory. The Bulgarians would take the southern part, including the towns of Bitola, Prilep, and Ohrid. The northern part of Macedonia was still a matter of dispute, but it was agreed that this territory would become a Russian protectorate until Serbia and Bulgaria finally reached an agreement over it.

The Bulgarians were aware that they should strive toward Macedonian autonomy because that would be just one step further from total annexation. In addition, the Bulgarians were satisfied with the agreement because they were sure Macedonia would become theirs. After all, Russia was their traditional ally and would make sure that Serbia followed their wishes. However, the Serbian side wasn't enthusiastic about the agreement. Nikola Pasic, a leader of the People's Radical Party of Serbia, strongly disagreed with the agreement since he considered Macedonia to be Serbian land. Although he became prime minister after the death of Milovan Milovanovic in 1912, Nikola Pasic didn't take any strong measures against the agreement with Bulgaria, but he continued to advocate against it.

While Bulgaria was negotiating with Serbia, it started reaching out to Greece. In May of 1912, the two states signed a treaty in Sofia by which they obliged themselves to provide political and military support against the Ottoman Empire; however, they never specified how they would divide the territories they gained once the Turks retreated from the Balkans. The Bulgarians avoided discussions of territorial division. They wanted Greece in the alliance because of their naval power and nothing else. The Balkan states had lost respect for the Greek army due to its failure to keep Crete. Thus, the Bulgarians were confident that their much larger and stronger army would be able to take over Macedonia before Greece set its claim on it.

During the summer of 1912, Greece concluded a "gentlemen's agreement" with Serbia and Montenegro. It was a non-formal, non-binding agreement, stating that these countries would help each other in their efforts against the Ottomans. Greece didn't manage to conclude an official agreement with Serbia before the outbreak of the war. This was mainly because Serbia needed Greece's assurance it would provide military help in case of an Austro-Hungarian attack. But Greece had no wish to meddle in the other problems of the Balkan nations since the only thing Greece had in common with them was animosity toward the Ottomans.

Eventually, all the states made agreements with each other and concluded the creation of the Balkan League. The Balkan League was an imperfect and flimsy construction, hastily put together for each involved country to reach its own self-interests. Nevertheless, the Balkan allies felt ready to fight the Ottomans and complete the process of national unity they had begun in the late 19th century. Ottoman control over the Balkan Peninsula had already deteriorated, and the Ottomans could no longer subdue the Albanian revolt. The war with Italy wasn't going well either, and the Young Turks started losing support. By August 1912, an anti-Young Turk movement rose to power and overthrew the Ottoman government.

War Preparations

Because the Balkan states were all pursuing their nationalistic goals, they needed large armies. Their military forces received a large portion of the national budget so they could become strong enough to challenge not only the Ottomans but also any constitutional or political restraints. The military generals never doubted their ability to successfully fight the Ottomans, and they worked hand in hand with the officers of their allied armies to achieve their common goal.

When the Balkan nations announced their mobilization, it was met with enthusiasm. Only some Serbian socialists and the Bulgarian Agrarian National Union remained skeptical. On the Ottoman side, no one looked forward to yet another war. The empire had recently been involved in wars in Yemen, North Africa, and Italy, and there was no patriotic enthusiasm left for a war with the Balkan states.

The Serbian and Bulgarian military staff often met to coordinate the attack. They signed a convention in Belgrade on April 29th, 1912, providing mutual defense efforts against Ottoman and Romanian attacks on Bulgarian territory and Austro-Hungarian attacks on Serbia. The next two agreements, which were signed on July 2nd and September 28th, provided the basis for the strategic conduct of the war. The Serbs tried to persuade the Bulgarians to send a large army to Macedonia or to the Vardar front, where they expected them to bring a decisive victory. But the Bulgarian generals argued that the main victory should be achieved in the Thracian front. General Ivan Fichev of the Bulgarian army managed to convince his Serbian counterpart that his plan was better. Thus, the main Bulgarian effort was to be in Thrace, while the main Serbian effort would be in Macedonia.

From a military perspective, this plan makes sense, as the Bulgarians had a large army that was capable of fighting the equally large Ottoman forces in the proximity of Constantinople. But politically, Macedonia was Bulgaria's major goal of the war, and with its forces so far away from it, Fichev risked losing Macedonia. He allowed the Serbian Army to occupy the parts of Macedonia that were to belong to Bulgaria as promised by the March convention, but that did not mean Fichev was unaware of the threat the Serbian Army posed to Bulgarian goals. Nevertheless, his priority was the defeat of the Ottoman Empire, and he acted appropriately. He hoped that the Bulgarian army could deal with the Serbian occupation of Macedonia later, and later on, Macedonia did become one of the main points of friction between the two Balkan states, which would lead to serious conflict later.

Bulgaria signed a convention with Greece on October 5th, 1912. This was after the call for mobilization, but it didn't matter because all that the Bulgarians needed was for Greece to ensure the Ottomans would not be able to transport men and arms to Europe by the Aegean Sea. They also agreed that they would not accept an armistice unless both parties approved. Bulgaria never put any hopes in the Greek army, believing that the war could be won even without the involvement of Greece. This is why they never sought any more agreements with Greece and left the question of southern Macedonia, especially the area around Thessaloniki, unresolved. The result would be overt hostility between the two Balkan states after the war was over. Serbia had no written convention with Greece, nor did Montenegro. Rather, they resorted to oral promises made with each other since Greece refused to sign a treaty that would put it in an unfavorable position if Austria-Hungary attacked Serbia.

Once all the alliances were achieved and after the mobilization of the army was ongoing, Bulgaria started demanding the implementation of Article 23 of the Treaty of Berlin, in which Macedonia was to be given autonomy. Bulgaria hoped this would make Macedonia easier to annex later on. The Ottoman Empire refused to grant the reforms that would give autonomy to its Balkan provinces, prompting the allies to prepare to attack.

The Great Powers did little to prevent the First Balkan War, which began on October 8th, 1912, with Montenegrin aggression on Ottoman positions. Six days later, Greece welcomed the Cretan delegates into the parliament, signaling their intention to join the war. The Ottoman Empire was provoked by the union of Crete and Greece, and it declared war on October 17th. The Balkan League responded, and the whole region exploded into a conflict that would rage for the next six years.

The Balkan Armies

The Balkan armies all followed the usual European model of training, communication, logistics, and sanitation, which made them very similar to each other. However, the Balkan armies were newer than the European ones, and they often invested in some older equipment. They preferred European manufactured weapons and machinery, but there was little to no standardization for the equipment. And as for the men that constituted the armies, the majority was made up of illiterate peasants who were indoctrinated with the appropriate nationalistic ideology. The armies were also very homogenous since only small numbers of ethnic minorities would join them. In general, the nations of the Balkan League didn't contain many minorities. Most of them were the Romani people, and they were not expected to serve, as they were deemed unreliable due to their nomadic way of life. The officers usually had foreign training and were professionals of different backgrounds.

The Bulgarian army was probably the one with the best training. It was often praised by foreign professionals, especially for its infantry and artillery. The Bulgarians also had the most modern weapons and good communication. Their officers were sent to Russia, Germany, or Italy to receive training. However, their main tactic was a French invention, and they strived to achieve a quick victory with a forceful attack. Greek and Serbian officers had similar backgrounds, with most of their officers being trained in Germany and Austria-Hungary.

The Bulgarians had a standing army of 60,000 men, but it easily increased to 350,000 when mobilization started. It had nine infantry divisions, whose men were armed with short bayonet rifles of European construction, and one cavalry division. Each infantry division had four machine-gun sections, with each having four 8-mm Maxim guns. The infantry also specialized in nighttime operations. Each division had a field artillery regiment attached to it, with nine batteries of four guns. They also had a significant number of older Krupp guns. Finally, the Bulgarians had a small navy with six torpedo boats and one 726-ton torpedo gunboat named *Nadezhda*. With this navy, they were able to protect their coastline on the Black Sea and prevent any blockage the Ottomans might impose on their communication with Russia. Just before the outbreak of the First Balkan War, the Bulgarian army owned five airplanes, but they quickly acquired seventeen more.

The Greek standing army counted 25,000 men, which grew to 110,000 during mobilization. They had four infantry divisions and six more battalions of Evzones (light infantry). The infantry units usually wielded 6.5-mm rifles. They also had field artillery attached to each division, which consisted of three groups of three four-gun batteries armed with 7.5-mm guns. They also had one heavy artillery battalion. In addition, the Greeks had three cavalry regiments and four airplanes. During the First Balkan War, they acquired three seaplanes to reinforce their navy, which was the pride of the Greek army. Of all the Balkan League nations, the Greeks had the biggest and best-organized navy, which they used to prevent the Ottomans from bringing men and weapons to the European front and to guard the Dardanelles. The Greek navy was also used to occupy the Aegean Islands, which were still under Ottoman control. Their most prized vessel was the 10,118-ton armored cruiser named *Georgios Averof,* which carried four 23-cm and eight 12-cm artillery guns. They also had sixteen destroyers, nineteen torpedo boats, and one submarine named *Delfin* ("Dolphin"). They also had smaller and older auxiliary vessels, as well as eleven thousand men serving in the navy under the command of Rear Admiral Pavlos Kuontouriotis.

The Montenegrin army was the smallest, and it lacked in equipment, training, and education of its officers. It was more a militia composed of almost all the country's males. It consisted of around thirty-six thousand men, who were armed with different varieties of guns of Russian production. They also had four batteries of light artillery and eight batteries of mountain artillery. Their small cavalry unit had only around thirty soldiers under the command of one officer. However, of all the Balkan League nations, only the Montenegrin army had recent experience in fighting a war. These nations continuously attacked the Montenegro-Ottoman border, providing each Montenegrin man with fighting experience. However, the Montenegrin soldiers never learned how to fight as an army or as a group. They were used to attacking and defending themselves as individuals.

Serbia had an army of 230,000 men divided into ten infantry divisions and one cavalry division. Each infantry regiment had a machine-gun section of four 7-mm guns. In total, the Serbs had around 228 7.5-mm quick-firing guns of European construction and some older Russian guns. They also had three planes, but they acquired seven more as the war progressed.

The Ottoman Empire was extremely large, and the countries of the Balkan League put together had fewer inhabitants than the empire. Of the twenty-six million people the Ottoman Empire had in total, six million lived in Europe. They were of various religious and ethnic backgrounds, which posed a threat to Ottoman unity. Most of them were Bulgarians, Serbs, Greek, and Albanians, and they felt little to no loyalty to the Ottoman Empire. Most of them were Orthodox Christians and would not fight against their brethren. There was a significant number of Asians (Arabs, Armenians, and Kurdish people) living in the European parts of the Ottoman Empire, but even they could not be expected to remain loyal to the European claims of the empire. The Ottoman army was very diverse, and the lack of sophisticated arrangements within the army made communication and training difficult. The soldiers didn't even speak the same language as their officers and had no sense of loyalty to the foreign commanders.

When the Young Turks took over the empire's government, they attempted to introduce changes into the army. British and German commanders were invited to oversee the reforms. However, it was the extent of the reforms that was the problem. The regular army was well trained and exceptionally organized, but the fighting in Europe would mainly rely on infantry reserves, which lacked training, equipment, competent leadership, and communication. Many officers of the reserves were non-Turks and non-Muslims. They had no loyalty toward the government in Constantinople, and once the war started, they often deserted. Only half of the Ottoman army was stationed in Europe. The rest was scattered in Asia, from Yemen to Anatolia, and in North Africa. Constantinople could have called on these armies to gain decisive numbers in the First Balkan War, but it still had difficulty transporting all the soldiers to European soil.

Chapter 3 – The First Balkan War: Thracian Theater

Bulgarian soldiers with dead Ottomans at their feet near Adrianople
https://en.wikipedia.org/wiki/First_Balkan_War#/media/File:Bulgaria
n_soldiers_with_dead_Turkish_civilians_(Edirne).jpg

The Outbreak of the War

Thrace was a major battlefield of the war because of its geography. It has very few natural obstacles and wide-open fields in which the armies were able to move without problems and bring the majority of their infantry and cavalry. Thrace was also important due to its proximity to Constantinople. This city was one of the main goals of the Balkan League since each nation was able to connect their national history to this place, although they would have to trace it far in the past when Constantinople was the capital of the Byzantine Empire. Despite all this, the Bulgarian army mostly fought in the Thracian theater against the Ottomans.

Aware of the situation in the Balkans, the Ottomans were the first to move their defensive army to Thrace (115,000 men) and Macedonia (175,000). The European forces of the Ottomans were in their respective places by September 24th, 1912. The leader of the Thracian Ottoman army was Abdullah Pasha, and the Macedonian Ottoman army was under the command of Ali Risa Pasha. They needed to construct a physical link between the two armies, and for that, they used the Kircaali detachment under the command of Yaver Pasha. They were stationed southwest of Adrianople. The Ottomans had their main garrison in Adrianople, which housed around fifty thousand soldiers. In Eastern Thrace, there was another garrison at Kirk Kilise (Lozengrad in Bulgarian). The Thracian theater was the most important front of the First Balkan War due to the size of the armies involved and the proximity of the Ottoman capital of Constantinople.

The Bulgarian commanders recognized that their frontier with Macedonia was unapproachable because of the high and unpredictable mountains. They knew that if they were to take Macedonia, it had to be done through Thrace. This is why they concentrated their army in this region as early as 1903. They were also aware that the Ottoman army had the numerical advantage since it had a larger army, which was why they could not risk the attack and had to come up with defensive tactics. Their primary goal was to prevent the Ottomans from reaching the Bulgarian capital of Sofia, and they were able to harass the Turks with rapid attacks and retreats. They had a small detachment stationed in the Rhodopes mountain region, where they could continuously harass the Ottomans and lay claim to Aegean Thrace. They also believed that the Turks would not attack this region because the terrain was difficult, and there were no roads by which they could easily transport troops and supplies for the army.

But all of this planning was dropped once the Italian-trained chief of staff, General Ivan Fichev, took command over the Thracian army. He insisted that both the western and eastern Thracian fronts should be offensive, as he suspected that the Ottomans would shift tactics in the prolonged war and move their Asian armies to Thrace. If they did that, the Bulgarians would be overwhelmed. Fichev knew that Bulgaria needed to achieve a quick victory in the Thracian theater, so he divided the Bulgarian forces into three armies. The 2nd Army was tasked with facing the main bulk of the Ottoman forces at Adrianople; however, they were ordered not to initiate the attack but to fight defensively. They didn't want to get involved in the siege of Adrianople since that would take time they didn't have. The 1st Army was stationed between Adrianople and Kirk Kilise, while the 3rd Army was to wait behind the Bulgarian cavalry division just northeast of the 1st Army.

The 1st Army was to initiate the attack, while the 3rd went around the Ottoman right flank and continued forward where they would take the fortress of Kirk Kilise. The 2nd Army was to keep the Adrianople garrison busy and prevent it from joining the rest of the Ottoman forces. The 1st and 3rd Armies were then to meet in an open battle against the Turks at Lule Burgas. But to achieve all this, the Bulgarian army needed to be precise and swift. The whole region between Adrianople and Kirk Kilise was open fields, so they would be easy targets for the Ottomans. Time was essential, and the Bulgarian army had to act quickly not only because the Turkish army had the numerical advantage but also because of the proximity of Anatolia, where the Turks stored their supplies. They also had a large population there that could be quickly mobilized and brought to fight the Bulgarians.

The success of the Balkan League in the First Balkan War entirely depended on the Thracian theater because if the Ottomans were to defeat the Bulgarians, there was nothing to stop them from moving westward and overwhelming the Greek, Serbian, and Montenegrin armies. The Bulgarians started moving toward Thrace on September 25th, 1912. At this point, they outnumbered the Ottomans. The 1st Army was under the command of General Vasil Kutinchev, while the 2nd was under General Nikola Ivanov. The 3rd Army was commanded by General Radko Dimitriev.

Bulgaria declared war on the Ottoman Empire on October 18th, 1912. On the same day they declared war, the Bulgarian troops moved across the Ottoman border. They needed to keep their plans secret, and when replying to questions from the foreign press, the Bulgarian leaders claimed their main goal was to take Adrianople. They were also aware that Turkey moved their army slowly and would not have all of its soldiers in place before November 1st.

Nevertheless, Abdullah Pasha of the Ottoman Empire ordered an offensive on October 21st before the whole army was in Thrace. He wanted to quickly envelop the Bulgarian frontier on the line from Adrianople to Kirk Kilise. The Ottomans wanted their offensive to be quick and stop the Bulgarian advance across the Tundzha River. They also wanted to demonstrate the success of the military reforms they introduced. Just as predicted, the Turks ignored the western units stationed at the Rhodope Mountains, thinking they were too small to achieve any significant gains. They wanted to concentrate their army in Eastern Thrace, where the terrain allowed them to engage in open battle. Trusting their numbers and military supremacy, they hoped they would achieve a quick victory that would assure the Ottomans' presence in Europe.

But the Ottomans' plan was ill-conceived. However, Abdullah Pasha would not be blamed for it. He only acted as he was commanded by the Ministry of War and its leader, Nizam Pasha, who ignored the advice of German General Colmar Von der Goltz. Other Ottoman officers were also against this hasty offensive but were unable to prevent it. The Ottomans were also oblivious of the Bulgarian army's strength, as they were confident in their success, even though many of their soldiers lacked equipment and were not prepared for the change from defensive to offensive tactics.

The Battle of Lozengrad (Kirk Kilise)

The Battle of Lozengrad was the first battle fought during the First Balkan War. It lasted for three days, from October 21st until October 24th, 1912. The front was thirty-six miles long, stretching from Lozengrad to Adrianople. The Ottomans had the fortress of Adrianople guarding their left flank, while the fortress of Lozengrad guarded their right flank. In between the fortresses, the corps of the 1st, 2nd, and 3rd Divisions, as well as the cavalry, covered the ground. They advanced to meet the Bulgarian 1st Army in the open field. At that time, the Bulgarian 2nd Army took its position near Adrianople to block the troops within the fortress garrison from helping their Ottoman comrades. The 3rd Army launched an infantry attack on the Ottomans stationed in the fortress of Lozengrad. They had the support of artillery units. The Lozengrad fortress wasn't as formidable as the one in Adrianople. Several days earlier, the German advisor to the Ottoman army, Field Marshal von der Goltz, claimed that Lozengrad would only be able to endure several months of siege. However, only one fort had a gun mounted on it. This wasn't nearly enough to fend off the advancing enemy troops.

The Bulgarian 1st Army faced the main force of the Ottoman Thracian army, but it managed to deflect the weak attack the Ottomans launched. Subsequently, they managed to move into a better position between Adrianople and the Ottoman cavalry division, allowing the Bulgarians to cut off any contact the cavalry could have with the fortress.

If the Ottomans had stronger leadership, they could have destroyed the right flank of the Bulgarian 1ˢᵗ Army with only one strong blow from the fortress. But the Ottomans didn't dare leave the safety of their garrison. Nizam Pasha intended to envelop the right flank of the Bulgarian 3ʳᵈ Army, but his attempt was easily parried. The Ottoman army stationed in Lozengrad panicked, and they abandoned the fortress on the evening of October 23ʳᵈ, retreating southeast.

The Battle of Lozengrad was the first time that the Bulgarians got the chance to demonstrate the power of their infantry troops. They were supported by artillery and chose to launch their attacks in poor light conditions, such as early dawn or even night. They were highly motivated, and their battle cry was "Na Nozh!" ("on a knife"). The success of their infantry was overwhelming, and many European military experts praised their tactics.

The ill-trained Ottoman troops were unable to endure the Bulgarian attacks along the line between Adrianople and Lozengrad, and they started a massive retreat on October 24ᵗʰ. Heavy rains only added to their demoralizing retreat, during which the soldiers often abandoned their weapons along the road. The Ottoman command, morale, and discipline had utterly failed. The Bulgarian army celebrated their first victory, which they achieved only six days after the start of the war.

The Turkish soldiers were terrified of the effectiveness of the modern Bulgarian artillery. They had around 1,500 dead and wounded, while around 3,000 Ottomans were taken as prisoners of war. On the Bulgarian side, 887 soldiers died, while 4,034 were wounded. Around 820 were reported missing in the area of Lozengrad.

Lule Burgas

After the victory at Lozengrad, the Bulgarian army was confident in their ability to defeat the Ottomans, and instead of chasing their fleeing enemy, they decided to rest. Even the cavalry rested instead of launching a scouting expedition to monitor the Turks. Thus, the Bulgarians lost contact with the Ottoman army, which proved to be a mistake. They could have followed the defeated Turks and achieved a total victory in Northern Thrace since the unorganized Ottoman army was near collapse. But the Bulgarians left the Turks to retreat in peace, which bought the Ottomans time to bring reinforcements from Constantinople. They also could take their time to dig shallow trenches along the ridge running from the Ergene River to the villages of Lule Burgas and Bunarhisar (modern-day Pinahisar). Here, they prepared a defense, with the artillery supporting the trenches. The new circumstances gave the Ottomans some morale and courage, allowing their officers to restore discipline.

Among the Bulgarian officers, only General Dimitriev was eager to pursue the Ottomans. He managed to convince the high command to order the forward march. Dimitriev's early attempts to initiate the attack were restrained by other officers who had concerns regarding the numbers of the Ottoman army. The Bulgarian high command wanted to play it safe, and they were very cautious, especially because the Ottoman army assumed a very strong defensive position. On October 27th, the Bulgarian army started its march forward. The overly enthusiastic commander of the 3rd Army pushed his troops in front, and they ended up being cut off from the rest of the army. Had they marched together, they would have been able to launch a quick and decisive attack on the still disorganized Ottomans.

The Ottoman reinforcements from Constantinople boosted the army's number to 130,000, which was around 20,000 more than what the Bulgarians had. Abdullah Pasha assumed the command of the 1st and 4th Corps positioned around Lule Burgas. The 2nd, 3rd, and 17th Corps were stationed around Bunarhisar, and they were under the command of Ahmed Hamdi Pasha. The new Ottoman soldiers who had just arrived in Thrace were fresh, well disciplined, and well trained. Abdullah Pasha conceived a plan to hold the line on his center and left and to use the right flank to go around the Bulgarian army, preventing it from maneuvering. The Bulgarian plan was to conduct a full-frontal attack by the 3rd Army, while the 1st Army went around the Ottoman left flank.

The Bulgarians attacked on October 29th, with their 3rd Army pounding on the Turkish ranks along the entire stretch from Lule Burgas to Bunarhisar. However, the 1st Army was delayed because of the bad weather, and it reached the battlefield a day later. The battle continued for the next four days, and the role of the artillery became very important on both sides. Nevertheless, the Turks held their position and fought much better than at Lozengrad. They even managed to force the Bulgarian army back to the middle of the line between the two villages, although not for long. Unfortunately, their logistics failed, and the artillery ended up not having enough shells to continue the attack.

This break in the artillery attack allowed the Bulgarian army to regroup and renew the attack. General Dimitriev came up with an idea to throw all of his troops into the battle at once. He also tried to sweep around the Ottoman right flank and block the Ottomans' retreat. Because of General Dimitriev's vigor and determination, the Bulgarian army prevailed, though it took them three days to break the Turkish defensive line.

On October 31st, the Ottoman left flank started faltering under the pressure of the Bulgarian 1st Army. In the center of the line, the Bulgarians advanced, separating the Ottoman forces. When the Bulgarian 3rd Army moved behind the Ottoman ranks, the same scenario as at Lozengrad occurred. The Turkish soldiers panicked and started retreating in disarray. The Bulgarian artillery concentrated on shelling the Ottoman infantry, as they had concluded early on that they should not waste their time trying to disable the Ottoman artillery since it was already ineffective. This bombardment made the Turkish soldiers demoralized due to the enormous losses they suffered.

The Battle of Lule Burgas is considered to be the largest and bloodiest battle of the First Balkan War, with the Bulgarians losing over twenty thousand men. The Ottomans had slightly greater losses, and around two thousand of their men were taken as prisoners. General Dimitriev deserved all the credit for the Bulgarian victory, but he was also responsible for the loss of so many soldiers. He was impatient, and he rushed to strike a decisive blow, sacrificing a significant portion of his army along the way.

The Ottomans lost two battles in just one week. Their morale was very low, especially since Thrace was wide open to the enemy, meaning the path to Constantinople had no obstacles. After the defeat at Lule Burgas, the Ottoman logistic system completely collapsed, especially because they had to rely on horses to haul equipment and supplies to their garrisons and battle lines. While retreating to the Ottoman capital, the Turkish soldiers had trouble finding food and shelter from the cold weather. There were no sanitary regulations among the troops, and cholera and dysentery soon appeared, reducing their numbers even more. The civilian refugees who fled the villages of Lule Burgas and Bunarhisar retreated to Constantinople together with the army. They were a burden, as there was not enough food and water for everyone, and they only served to spread the diseases around the military camps.

Just as before, the Bulgarians failed to pursue their enemy, but this time, the price they had to pay for it was much higher. Had they sent their cavalry to harass the retreating Ottomans, they could have completely broken their morale and organization. This would, in turn, have led them to a defenseless Constantinople, which they would have been able to take without much trouble. But the cavalry, who didn't take part in much of the fighting at Lule Burgas, claimed they were tired and needed rest. The Bulgarian army rested for five days before following the Ottomans. This allowed Constantinople to move its

Anatolian army and organize a new defensive line some twenty miles west of the capital.

The Chataldja Line

The 1st and 3rd Bulgarian Armies were the first to start moving toward Constantinople. They took their time to reach the antique fortifications of Chataldja (also known as Catalca), which was named after a nearby village. These fortifications weren't only a military problem for the Bulgarians but also a political one. The government in Sofia was against the attack on Chataldja and on Constantinople because that would anger the Russians, who wanted to claim the imperial capital and thus take control over the Bosporus. They didn't want the Bulgarians to infringe on the matters of Constantinople. The Bulgarian leaders were aware of the Russian sentiment, but they also knew that taking Constantinople would mean an advantage in the war. They would be in a position to dictate the terms of the peace. Tsar Ferdinand even planned a theatrical entrance into the Ottoman capital, and Germany and Austria-Hungary did nothing to prevent it from happening.

But the possibility of losing Constantinople put the Ottoman Empire on edge. The Muslim inhabitants posed a serious threat to the Christians who resided in the capital. To prevent a massacre, the Great Powers sent an international fleet into the Bosporus to preserve the peace. Germany, Great Britain, Austria-Hungary, Italy, Spain, the Netherlands, and Romania sent their ships and soldiers on November 18th to Constantinople. But not everyone thought that the Great Powers should meddle. The American attaché to Constantinople stated that the city remained calm even though the Bulgarian army was approaching. However, not even he could claim that everything would remain peaceful if the Bulgarians entered the city.

At the Chataldja fortifications, the Bulgarian army encountered a problem. They did not anticipate coming this far, and they didn't know anything about the fortifications and what threat they posed to their army. The latest information they had about this defensive point was dated to 1906, and it proved to be useless. The defensive line of Chataldja stretched around thirty miles from the shores of the Black Sea to the Sea of Marmara. The designer of the fortifications was a German engineer, von Bluhm Pasha, who entered Ottoman service in 1877. The forts were hill-crested redoubts that fell out of use since their initial construction in 1878, but they were renovated on several occasions. The redoubts consisted of trenches and artillery guns behind which heavy artillery was mounted with batteries forming several lines. Each redoubt ended with natural obstacles, such as estuaries, swamps, or lakes. This combination of natural and man-made obstacles was very formidable, and it gave the Ottoman army a much better position than it had at Lozengrad or Lule Burgas.

The Ottoman soldiers found new motivation to fight, for they knew that if Chataldja were lost, Constantinople would be next. The new soldiers brought from the edges of Anatolia were well rested and eager to fight. They amounted to around 100,000 men and 280 artillery pieces. The 3rd Corps assumed the position in the northern flank (the Black Sea), while the 2nd Corps assumed the middle lines. The 1st Corps represented the southern flank (Sea of Marmara). The commander of the Chataldja defense was Nizam Pasha, but on November 4th, the military high command sent Mahmud Muhtar Pasha to lead the 3rd Corps. His appearance boosted the morale of the Turkish soldiers because he had been severely wounded at the Battle of Lozengrad but made a full recovery by the time of the Battle of Chataldja. He was also the son of the grand vizier and war hero of the Russo-Turkish War, Ahmed Muhtar Pasha.

On November 12th, while the Bulgarian army advanced toward Chataldja, Tsar Ferdinand received the Ottoman request for an armistice. This could have ended the war, but the tsar thought of Constantinople as the perfect imperial prize that would bring him enormous prestige. He needed the war to continue, and he refused an armistice with the excuse that he alone could not make such a decision in the name of Bulgaria. On November 14th, he issued the order to his armies to attack Chataldja. But at that point, not all of the Bulgarian armies had arrived at their positions. Fortunately, the chiefs of the general staff, Ivan Fichev and Mihail Savov, advised against the premature attack.

General Dimitriev, who was on the field, patiently awaited the order to attack. His troops were tired, and dysentery and cholera started spreading through the Bulgarian camps. The sanitary system of the Bulgarian army was overwhelmed. On November 17th, the forces listed 29,719 soldiers suffering from cholera. Out of that number, 4,615 died. The Ottomans suffered from the diseases as well, but they were only twenty miles away from their capital, so they had access to medicine and care. The Bulgarian army, on the other hand, was far away from home, at the end of their supply train, and had no proper medical care. Any attack they would launch at this point would be difficult.

Nevertheless, the Bulgarian military leaders felt obliged to push for the attack. They believed that no sacrifice was too great for Bulgaria to take over Constantinople. However, they allowed nationalistic sentiment to triumph over logic. Their forces had been reduced by the hardship of war and illness, and they were exhausted by the march through a territory without proper railways or roads. Nevertheless, the order to attack arrived on November 16th, and General Dimitriev drew up a plan. The Bulgarian army was to attack the whole defensive Ottoman line, with the 1st Army charging on the southern part while the 3rd Army took the north. The artillery was to cover the attack with constant bombardments.

The attack began on the foggy morning of November 17th. The Bulgarians hoped the fog would provide them with cover, but it proved to be more of a nuisance since it interrupted communication between the armies, preventing the proper coordination of the attack. Nevertheless, the artillery started shooting, and the bombardment could be heard all the way in Constantinople. The Bulgarians easily advanced a couple of hundred yards toward the Ottoman line, but they were soon overwhelmed by the Turkish artillery. In the Sea of Marmara, the Ottoman battlecruiser *Mecidiye* and battleship *Barbaros Hayreddin* were stationed. They had 8- and 12-inch guns mounted on their decks, which they used to bombard the Bulgarian infantry.

The Bulgarian army was now pinned down and could not advance. Nevertheless, they continued to fight throughout the night of November 18th, during which a battalion from the 3rd Army managed to surprise and occupy one fortified position in the northern sector of the defense line. Unfortunately, the Bulgarians failed to exploit this success, which might have brought them victory. The fog lingered for days and obstructed military communication. They were soon discovered, and the Ottoman barrage turned on them, forcing the Bulgarian soldiers to abandon the position. Realizing how futile the attack was, General Dimitriev ordered it to be discontinued in the afternoon of November 18th. The next day, the Bulgarian army withdrew and formed a defensive line of their own, right in front of the Ottoman line.

The Battle of Chataldja was their first defeat of the First Balkan War, and they lost around three thousand men, with another nine thousand being wounded. The Ottomans had a similar number of casualties, but they remained firmly in their positions. The Bulgarian army's failure can be explained by the low visibility, which prevented the artillery from giving its best. Some of them even fired on their own retreating troops. The lack of communication, as well as cholera and dysentery, were demoralizing, to say the least. They numbered only 85,597 battle-ready men, and it was clear to General Dimitriev that no success would come out of further actions taken at Chataldja.

On the other hand, the Ottoman army, which was supported by the artillery from two battleships, proved to be superior. They brought in fresh troops from Anatolia, and although they, too, suffered the diseases, it was somewhat under control. The proximity to Constantinople also gave them the advantage of having fresh food supplies, as well as a good communication line with their high command. The fighting continued through November 22nd and 23rd, but no side claimed victory. Both armies were exhausted by then and were in no position to launch an offensive attack. The effort at Chataldja ended in a stalemate.

Adrianople

The city of Adrianople was the most important Ottoman position in Thrace because it was fortified. It was also the second-largest city after Constantinople. Despite this, the Bulgarians never saw this city as their goal. It had only a small number of Bulgarians living in it, and it had no political or cultural importance to the Bulgarian state. Nevertheless, the Ottomans believed they would have to defend Adrianople, so they stationed most of their artillery there, as well as a significant portion of their army. There were 52,597 soldiers in the city and 340 artillery guns of various types. The Ottomans were sure of the defensive capabilities of the city, and they could never have imagined a force passing Adrianople in their advance toward Constantinople.

At first, the Bulgarians didn't want to attack Adrianople. There are several reasons for this. In 1909, they sent an ambassador to the city, who worked undercover to investigate the city's defenses. But by the time the war broke out in 1912, this information was already old. The Bulgarian leaders didn't know how many guns and men the Ottomans had brought to the city. They were aware that these numbers must have been great since they knew the empire considered Adrianople one of the most important ones. The other problem was Russia. Even though taking Adrianople would bring Bulgaria a great advantage, they didn't want to anger their Russian allies who helped them to achieve independence in the first place. The Russians claimed Adrianople as a city under their sphere of influence since it was so close to the Bosporus, a strait they eagerly wanted to control. However, on November 4th, 1912, the Russian ambassador in Sofia notified the Bulgarian leaders that St. Petersburg would no longer object to the

Bulgarian annexation of Adrianople. Russia did this because it was impressed with the Bulgarian army's might and wanted to please its leaders so the alliance between the two countries would remain firm.

The Bulgarians were elated by Russia's permission to acquire Adrianople. Inspired by the victories at Lozengrad and Lule Burgas, the Bulgarian army started preparing for the siege of the city even before they received the green light from Russia or Sofia. Just as their armies started their attack on Lule Burgas on October 29th, the Bulgarian high command decided to launch an attack on Adrianople. The 2nd Army, enhanced by the addition of the 2nd Division, encircled the city. On October 31st, an independent cavalry and the infantry of the 8th Division occupied Dimotika, just southwest of Adrianople. With this, they also cut off the city from Constantinople, preventing communication between the Ottoman forces.

The Bulgarians also invited their Serbian allies to help with the siege of Adrianople. Serbia had previously achieved a victory at Kumanovo (which will be discussed later), and they overran Macedonia and were in a position to move their forces to Thrace. Serbian General Stepa Stepanovic moved his 2nd Army on October 30th so the siege could start. The Serbians provided the Bulgarian army with 47,275 additional men and 72 artillery guns. By November 9th, the 2nd Bulgarian and Serbian Armies tightened their grip on Adrianople, ensuring that the Ottomans could not break out and escape. The artillery bombardment of Adrianople started as early as October 29th, but the Bulgarians and Serbians didn't have enough guns or men to do anything more than threaten the Ottomans.

The Ottomans within Adrianople were aware of the Bulgarian army approaching. They did not remain idle; they tried on several occasions to push their way out of the city by launching attacks on their enemies. However, they were unsuccessful. In the last attempt to break through, which was conducted on October 29th, the Ottomans lost 1,200 men to the Bulgarian artillery.

When Bulgaria lost the Battle of Chataldja, Adrianople became increasingly important. They started the heavy bombardment of the city and even brought planes and balloons to coordinate attacks. The Bulgarian leaders hoped that the bombardment would create tension in the city, making it an easier target. The bombardment continued until the end of November, when the Ottoman commanders decided to capitulate. Even during the negotiations of the armistice, Tsar Ferdinand ordered a renewed attack on the city. He hoped he would force more favorable conditions for the conclusion of peace. But the members of the general staff persuaded the tsar to give up on a new attack because they already promised no military activity during the negotiations. The negotiations were not fruitful, and the siege of Adrianople continued until March 26th, 1913, when the Bulgarians finally entered the city and claimed it. The fall of Adrianople was a decisive battle, and it would bring an end to the First Balkan War.

The Western Thrace Front

The Bulgarian army sent a small force of only twenty-five thousand men, under the command of General Stiliyan Kovachev, to Western Thrace. These forces were further divided into the Haskovo Detachment and the Rhodope Detachment. The Ottomans stationed their Kircaali Detachment in this region, which totaled around thirty thousand men under the command of Yaver Pasha. These Ottoman forces failed to stop the invading Bulgarians and were forced to retreat southeast early on during the Bulgarian attacks.

The Haskovo Detachment moved to take the city of Kardzhali. As soon as they conquered it, a part of the detachment moved to help the Bulgarian and Serbian 2nd Armies at Adrianople. The part that remained in the city assumed the name Kardzhali Detachment and continued to the Aegean port city of Dedeagach. They were surprised to find that the Bulgarian irregulars of the Macedonian-Thracian Legion were already in control of the port. By November 27th, the Rila Infantry Division of the Bulgarian army arrived at Dedeagach on their way to Eastern Thrace. The Kardzhali Detachment joined them.

The Bulgarian army's presence cut the communication lines between Constantinople and the Ottoman Macedonian army. The Bulgarian units then moved to occupy the northern shore of the Sea of Marmara and the Gallipoli Peninsula. They pursued the Ottoman army to Southern Thrace, and they stopped at the village of Merhamli. After a brief battle, Yaver Pasha surrendered his force of around ten thousand Ottoman soldiers.

The Rhodope Detachment was divided into three so they could cross the Ottoman-Bulgarian border in three different places. The 1st Division took the Temrosh salient and the town of Smolyan. From there, they had easy access to Dedeagach. The 2nd Division crossed the border at Batak in Bulgaria, and on October 30th, it took the Ottoman city of Nevrokop (today's Gotse Delchev, Bulgaria). On November 5th, they also took Drama. The 3rd Division moved from Rakitovo to Bansko and joined the 2nd Division at Nevrokop.

All of the Rhodope divisions were highly trained mountaineers, capable of moving quickly over difficult terrain. By the end of October, they were able to occupy the whole Rhodopes, and they encountered little resistance from the Ottomans or the native Pomaks, the Bulgarian-speaking Muslims. The Ottoman forces were left at Adrianople and Chataldja, but they were chased away from the Aegean seaboard. Although there was very little fighting in the Rhodopes, the Bulgarian army that took the region concluded the occupation of Thrace.

Chapter 4 – The First Balkan War: Western Theater

Serbian Army commander Crown Prince Alexander (left) and Chief of Staff Petar Bojovic (sitting next to Crown Prince)

https://en.wikipedia.org/wiki/Battle_of_Kumanovo#/media/File:Serbia n_1st_Army_Staff_1st_Balkan_War.jpg

Serbian Efforts

The Serbian Army was divided into four main groups. The 1st Army was under the direct command of Crown Prince Alexander Karadjordjevic. This was also the largest Serbian force, numbering over 130,000 men. They were stationed in the Lower Morava Valley. The Serbian 2nd Army was commanded by General Stepa Stepanovic, and it numbered around seventy-four thousand men and was stationed in southwestern Bulgaria, from where it could easily cross into Macedonia. The 2nd Army consisted of the Danube Division and the Bulgarian 7th Rila Division. The Serbian 3rd Army numbered around seventy-six thousand men and was under the command of General Bozidar Jankovic. It was also divided into two groups, one concentrated at Toplica and the second at Medvedje. The fourth group of the Serbian forces was actually two armies. The Ibar Army, which consisted of twenty-five thousand men, was under the command of General Mihailo Zivkovic, and the twelve thousand men of the Javor Brigade were commanded by Colonel Milivoje Andjelkovic.

The chief of staff of the Serbian Army was General Radomir Putnik, and he planned the all-out attack on the Ottomans. The Serbian military leaders believed that the Ottomans would concentrate their forces around the Morava and Vardar Rivers in central Macedonia. The Serbian 1st Army was to attack the Turks directly, occupying the Morava and Vardar Valleys in the process. This would break not only the Ottoman control of central Macedonia but also establish a Serbian presence in the contested region. The Serbian 3rd Army was tasked with occupying southern Kosovo, from where they would enter Macedonia and attack the Ottoman left flank. The meeting point of the first three Serbian armies would be Ovce Pole, just east of Skopje. The general staff thought this would be the point where a clash with the main Ottoman army would occur.

The Ibar Army and the Javor Brigade were tasked with entering the Sanjak of Novi Pazar from the south and north, respectively. While the Ibar Army needed to occupy the city of Novi Pazar, the Javor Brigade had to monitor the activities of Austria-Hungary and prevent it from meddling. If the Habsburgs failed to react, the Javor Brigade would move north of Sanjak to help with the occupation. The Serbian plan was developed to bring a quick and decisive victory, but it depended on the rapid movement of the armies. Good coordination with the Greek and Montenegrin armies, as well as the Bulgarian efforts in Thrace, would ensure an Ottoman defeat.

The Ottoman army in the western theater numbered around 175,000 men, and they were stationed in Macedonia and what is today Albania. This army was larger than its Thracian counterpart, but unlike the Thracian force, the European Ottoman army couldn't be reinforced with Anatolian detachments due to the Greek navy blocking the Aegean Sea. The Ottomans, therefore, depended on Albanian irregulars, and they even supplied them with sixty-three thousand rifles. At this point, the Albanians thought Ottoman rule would be preferable due to cultural similarities between the two people.

The main strategy of the Ottoman army in the western theater was to hold on to their positions and wait. They hoped their Thracian army would win a swift victory over the Bulgarians and be able to send Anatolian reinforcements into Europe. They would also provide defense for the very important Thessaloniki-Constantinople railroad, which supplied the army and provided communication. The only strong position the Ottomans had in the west was in Albania.

Kumanovo

The Serbian 1st Army crossed to Macedonia on October 19th, 1912. Three days later, they encountered the Ottoman Vardar Army, which was led by Zeki Pasha. They numbered around fifty-eight thousand men, which was less than half of the Serbian army that was approaching. Nevertheless, the size of the Ottoman army was a surprise for Serbian General Putnik, as he didn't believe they would be concentrated in such numbers, especially so early during the war. The Serbs hoped the first major battle would take place in southern Macedonia, where they would meet their other armies.

The Ottomans were the first to take action. On the early morning of October 23rd, Zeki Pasha launched an attack on the Serbian right flank. The Ottoman army was more numerous at this point because not all of the divisions of the Serbian Army arrived at the battlefield. The Serbs also had trouble bringing their artillery into position due to underdeveloped logistics. As soon as each division arrived on the battlefield, it immediately engaged in combat. The Serbian soldiers charged into the battle willingly, not even allowing themselves a rest after the long march. But after the first day of the fighting was over, Zeki Pasha was confident in an Ottoman victory.

The next day, the Serbian Army decided to launch a counterattack since more of its units arrived on the battlefield. By the morning of October 24th, the artillery started arriving and provided the infantry with protection. Finally, the Serbian artillery overwhelmed the Ottomans and allowed its infantry to charge into an open attack.

The Ottoman artillery lacked the forward observers who would help direct the bombing. Furthermore, they failed to act as one army, and their artillery did not protect the infantry. Even though eighteen new artillery pieces had arrived from Skopje, Zeki Pasha failed to position them where they would be most effective. This additional firepower would have helped the Ottomans defeat the Serbian army, but their commander's failure led to the early retreat of the Turkish army. Their soldiers were prone to panic, and they abandoned their positions, allowing the Serbs their first victory.

The Serbs lost around 1,000 men and had 3,208 wounded. The Ottoman casualties were much greater, amounting to twelve thousand dead. Only three hundred were taken as prisoners. King Peter of Serbia was surprised by the victory because his army was initially caught by surprise. In celebration, he awarded General Radomir

Putnik with the title of voivode (a field marshal, which was the highest military rank in Serbia). The victory of the Battle of Kumanovo brought northern parts of Macedonia under Serbian control. This meant that Serbia now had the advantage over the territory in the dispute against Bulgaria. They were also unlikely to give it away willingly since they had sacrificed their men to take it.

The Ottomans began the Battle of Kumanovo with an aggressive attack, hoping they would be able to break the Serbian ranks early during the war. But they didn't have the numbers that would help them sustain the attack. In general, the Ottoman artillery was as ineffective in Macedonia as it was in Thrace, which made Nizam Pasha in Constantinople realize the flaws of his strategies. Modern military experts claim that the Ottomans should have never engaged the Serbian Army so far north in Vardar Valley. Instead, they should have mounted a defensive action to the south at Bitola. There, they would have uninterrupted communication with Albanian forces that could have quickly come to help. This defensive line could have been guarded for a prolonged time and maybe even bring about an Ottoman victory if the Anatolian reinforcements ever arrived.

The Ottomans retreated to Bitola in panic. One soldier, angered by the defeat, attempted to assassinate Zeki Pasha, but he only managed to add to the overwhelming panic that ensued in the Turkish army. They didn't even attempt to defend Skopje, abandoning many guns and other military equipment there. If they had formed a defense near Skopje, they would have at least slowed down the Serbian advance southward.

Voivode Putnik sent the main part of the 1st Army and a smaller division from the 3rd Army to pursue the fleeing Ottomans to Bitola. Another division was instructed to follow the disorganized Turks to Veles. However, they failed to send most of their army to pursue the Ottomans. If they had done so, they would have been able to crush the Vardar force in central Macedonia and end the Macedonian effort two weeks earlier.

Prilep

The Serbian Army moved southward, but because of the bad roads, they could not march together. Instead, the Morava Division went ahead, followed by the Drina Division. Upon approaching the city of Prilep, the Ottomans, under the command of Kara Said Pasha, attacked the Morava Division. The battle would last for the next three days.

The Serbian Army was unable to do much but sit and wait for their compatriots to arrive. But once the Morava and Drina Divisions were united, the Serbs gained the advantage, and they pushed the Ottoman 5th Corps south of the city. By November 5th, the Serbian Army was ready to start moving south again, but they again found themselves under fire. The Serbian officers decided that an attack would be the best defense. They had no artillery following them, so they organized the infantry to engage in a large-scale attack. The Turks were surprised by this bold move, and they were even impressed by the discipline of the Serbian soldiers, a discipline the Ottomans had failed to install in their army. The Serbs fought vigorously in close combat, using bayonets and hand grenades. But these open battle charges left the soldiers vulnerable, and even though the tactic was successful, many Serbs had to sacrifice their lives.

The Serbian 1st Army didn't have its main commander, Crown Prince Alexander. During the Battle of Kumanovo, he fell ill due to the cold and hardship of army life. Nevertheless, he maintained regular telephone contact with his troops from his sickbed in Skopje.

The sheer size and enthusiasm of the Serbian Army were enough to overwhelm the Turks. But the Ottomans still managed to demonstrate their ability to fight a mighty enemy, and they harassed the Serbian Army with quick attacks. The Ottomans lost around 1,200 men in the battle, while Serbian casualties counted over 2,000. Nevertheless, they were successful in defeating the Turks and opening the way south to Bitola.

Because the Bulgarian leaders never constructed a territorial agreement concerning Macedonia with Greece, they had to rely on Serbia to occupy Bitola before the Greek army could get to the city. The Bulgarians trusted the Serbians because the two countries signed a territorial agreement that was guaranteed by Russia. Luckily, the Greeks didn't pay much attention to Bitola, mainly because they had their eye on Thessaloniki. The Serbians were happy to oblige because if they conquered the whole of Macedonia, their claim on its western part would be confirmed. Thus, on November 8th, the Serbian high command ordered an advance on Bitola.

The Serbian Army approached the city in two groups. The first one came from the northwest, while the second group moved from the northeast. The cavalry guarded the army's left flank and scouted ahead. However, the Serbian artillery was not yet in place. The Ottomans had destroyed the railroad from Veles to Bitola, and the roads were muddy due to heavy rains and generally bad weather.

After the Battle of Kumanovo, much of the Ottoman army retreated to Bitola. There, they established a defensive line, which would turn out to be their last stand in Macedonia. The Vardar Ottoman army was scattered around the city, while the 7th Corps held the left flank. The 6th Corps was in the center, and the 5th corps had the right flank. The overall command was still in the hands of Zeki Pasha, and he had the help of the Kochana and Ioannina independent divisions. Overall, the Vardar Army numbered only around thirty-eight thousand men and one hundred artillery pieces. The Serbs had 108,544 soldiers approaching Bitola but lacked artillery, which was still being dragged along the muddy roads. Because of the numerical disadvantage, the Ottomans decided to establish their strongest position in the Oblakov heights.

The Ottomans opened fire on the Serbian Army on the morning of November 16th. At that point, some of the Serbian guns arrived, and they were able to respond to the fire, at least somewhat. Then, the

Serbian infantry charged forward; many units went without the coverage of artillery.

To break the Ottoman resistance, the Serbian Army had to reach Oblakov and destroy the strongest spot of the Ottoman defense. They achieved this on November 17th, and the next day, the rest of the Serbian artillery arrived. This was enough to achieve victory, as the heavy artillery was able to single out and destroy the Ottoman batteries. The right flank of the Serbian Army was now able to push past the Turkish defenses, causing the whole Ottoman army to break into a retreat. Just as before, the Ottoman soldiers gave in to panic, and the retreat was disorganized and hasty.

The Vardar Army suffered two major defeats in just one week, and this was a blow to the morale of the Ottoman soldiers. In the Battle of Bitola, the Turks lost more than one thousand men, while over two thousand were wounded and five thousand were taken as prisoners. Serbian casualties counted around five hundred dead and two thousand wounded. After yet another defeat, over five thousand soldiers of the Vardar Army deserted. After the Battle of Bitola, the Turkish armies were forced to leave Macedonia and find a place to retreat to in Albania.

On November 19th, the Serbs entered the conquered city, proclaiming their control over southwestern Macedonia. This meant they also laid claim on Ohrid, which was a symbolically important town for the Serbs, Bulgarians, and Greeks. The Battle of Bitola ended the five-century-long Ottoman rule of Macedonia, and it also ended the fighting for a large part of the Serbian Army. Although some Serbian leaders wanted their army to continue southward to Salonika, Voivode Radomir Putnik refused to advance. Serbia was still under the threat of war with Austria-Hungary, and the Serbians needed their army closer to their capital of Belgrade.

The Serbian 2nd and 3rd Armies didn't fight much at all. The troops under Commander Stepa Stepanovic crossed the border from Macedonia together with the 7th Rila Division of the Bulgarian army.

They met very little Ottoman resistance and were able to swiftly deal with the Turks at Kochana in the Vardar Valley.

After occupying Kochana, the Bulgarian high command ordered the Rila Division to move to Thessaloniki, where they would continue fighting. The Belgrade high command sent the order to Stepanovic to move one of his divisions to Thrace and help the Bulgarians with the siege of Adrianople. He led his army to Thrace on October 27th, and they would spend the next five months there.

The Serbian 3rd Army was attacked early on during the First Balkan War by the Albanian irregulars, but they were able to take Pristina and Kosovo by October 22nd. The Serbian Army's entry into Pristina played a significant role in elevating nationalistic spirit since, in a way, this was their homecoming. In the medieval period, Kosovo was the most important land of the Kingdom of Serbia, as it was where the famous Battle of Kosovo took place. Pristina was the Serbian capital of the Nemanjic dynasty.

On October 23rd, part of the Serbian 3rd Army moved to Skopje. The other part moved through central Albania to reach the Adriatic Sea. Their arrival to the coast met strong diplomatic opposition from Austria-Hungary, which wanted to prevent Serbia from gaining access to the sea since they thought Serbia would present a threat to their dominion over the Adriatic.

On October 20th, the Javor Brigade moved to Sanjak, where it met the Montenegrin army. They didn't encounter much resistance at Novi Pazar. They then continued to the town of Sjenica, which they took on October 25th. By the end of the month, the whole Sanjak of Novi Pazar was in the hands of the Serbian and Montenegrin armies, and the two countries finally achieved physical contact for the first time since the Treaty of San Stefano in 1878.

The Montenegrin Efforts

Albanian soldiers at Scutari
https://sh.wikipedia.org/wiki/Opsada_Skadra#/media/Datoteka:Albani
an_soldiers_(Siege_of_Shkod%C3%ABr).jpg

The Montenegrin army had only two major goals in the First Balkan War. One was the annexation of the Sanjak of Novi Pazar and Kosovo, and the other one was to obtain the city of Scutari (today Shkodër) in northern Albania. This city was especially important for the Montenegrins, who were from the mountainous region and barely had a viable economy. Instead, they depended on foreign subsidies. If they could take control of Scutari and the whole region around it (Scutari Vilajet), they would be able to develop an independent economy.

The Montenegrins divided their forces into three groups. The Eastern Division was under the command of Janko Vukotic and counted around twelve thousand men. They had thirty-two guns with them. Their goal was to take the Sanjak of Novi Pazar, from where they would march to Prizren and take Kosovo. Other Montenegrin armies were concentrated around Scutari, which was separated from Montenegro by Lake Scutari. Crown Prince Danilo led the Zeta

Division, which consisted of fifteen thousand men and forty guns. They approached the city from the eastern shore of the lake. Brigadier Mitar Martinovic commanded the Coastal Division, which numbered eight thousand men and thirty-four guns. They were reinforced by a group of volunteers of around five hundred men. As a whole, the Montenegrin armies were under the supreme command of King Nikola I Petrovic-Njegos, as was the custom among the Balkan nations.

Montenegro was the first to engage the Ottomans in the battle of all the members of the Balkan League. The Ottomans had around 13,600 soldiers and 96 guns in their Scutari Corps, and they were waiting to defend the city from the Montenegrin attack. They were under the command of Hasan Riza Bey, but they were not alone. Esad Pasha Toptani brought the Albanian reserves to help defend this important city. The area around Scutari was hilly, and the presence of a lake made this point very strong for organizing a defense. The Ottomans fortified the hills of Tarabosh, Brda, and Bardanjolt; the northern side of the city was an open field.

The Siege of Scutari

Ever since the first days of the war, the Zeta Division of the Montenegrin army had encountered the Ottomans in small battles while they moved toward the eastern shore of Lake Scutari. Once they reached the shore, the army had to rest because the Ottomans had harassed them for five days without pause. This allowed the Turkish leaders to organize the city's defense and bring eight thousand additional soldiers from the surrounding areas.

The Zeta Division launched their first attack on October 18th, the same day the other allies of the Balkan League officially entered the war. The Coastal Division of the Montenegrin army moved along the west shore of the lake. Unlike the Zeta Division, the Coastal Division encountered only light Ottoman resistance, so the soldiers were rested and ready to launch an attack as soon as they approached Scutari.

The active siege of the city started once both divisions were in place, with the Zeta Division just north of the city of Scutari, while the Coastal Division was in the west, at the base of the Tarabosh hill. The Zeta Division tried to rush the city and take it on October 24th, but it failed due to the Ottomans' determined resistance. The renewed attack came on October 28th when the men of the Zeta Division tried to outflank the open area in the north. Instead, they attacked the Bardanjolt hill to the east. They managed to take the hill but failed to hold it. The Ottoman counterattack dislodged the Montenegrins from Bardanjolt, forcing them to retreat and reorganize.

The Montenegrins had trouble taking Scutari because they lacked an organized command. Instead, they attacked the city individually, and although their artillery bombarded the city, it never offered protection for the infantry. That is why they had a high number of casualties. The Coastal Division was mainly inactive while the Zeta Division launched its futile attacks. Upon seeing this, Hasan Riza Bey decided to move the troops he stationed at the Tarabosh hill to help in the city's defense. The Montenegrins also didn't have enough men to surround the city, and they left its southern end open, allowing the Ottomans to get supplies and reinforcements. By mid-November, the Ottomans reinforced their defense with an additional twenty-four thousand men.

The Serbian advance into northern Albania brought some relief to the Montenegrins. On November 18th, parts of the Serbian 3rd Army made contact with the Montenegrin Coastal Division at Alessio. Once they took this town, they managed to close the gap in the siege of Scutari. The city was finally surrounded, but it wasn't enough. The Ottomans still managed to defend their position. Encouraged by the Ottoman defeats in Thrace, Macedonia, and Kosovo, Crown Prince Danilo of Montenegro decided to push for yet another attempt to take Scutari. He was afraid that Austria-Hungary would meddle and take the whole area to create an independent Albanian state. However, King Nikola wanted to try to take the city through diplomatic means.

When the armistice was signed on December 3rd, 1912, Scutari remained in the hands of the Ottoman Empire. The Montenegrins continued with the siege, cutting the city off from receiving provisions. The situation was a complete stalemate; the Montenegrins didn't have enough men to take the city, and the Ottomans couldn't break the siege. But the Montenegrins were aware that they needed to be patient. The Serbian Army was done fighting for Macedonia and was free to come and reinforce the siege with both men and artillery.

Other Operations of the Montenegrin Forces

The Eastern Division of the Montenegrin army entered the Sanjak of Novi Pazar only one day after the formal proclamation of the war. The division was further divided into three detachments, which were sent in three different directions. The first detachment moved north, where they took Bijelo Polje on October 11th and Berane on October 16th. The second detachment moved toward Plav and Gusinje, entering these towns on October 20th and 23rd, respectively. But near Chakor, they encountered serious Ottoman resistance under the command of Djavid Pasha. Nevertheless, the Montenegrin army managed to force the Ottomans to retreat. Both of these detachments moved to Kosovo, where they were divided into three columns. Two of them took Pec on November 2nd and then joined with the third column to take Decani. From there, the united army marched to the south toward Gjakova, which was an important trade town at the time.

The third detachment of the Montenegrin Eastern Division entered the northern Sanjak of Novi Pazar, where it remained stationary because the reactions of Austria-Hungary had to be observed. Once it was clear that the Habsburgs wouldn't send their army, this detachment moved to meet the Serbian Javor Brigade on October 28th. Together, they took the town of Pljevlja.

Of all the Balkan League members, Montenegro was the only one that didn't have any initial success against the Ottomans. Most of their army was stuck at Scutari, engaging in a futile siege of the city. But they did succeed in taking over the western parts of Sanjak without major problems. Even then, Sanjak was shared with Serbia. Both Montenegro and Serbia were Serbian states, and they wanted Prizren, a medieval capital of the Kingdom of Serbia. From this city, they would be able to assert dominance over the Serbian lands more easily. However, by the time the Montenegrin army achieved all of its goals and was able to move, the Serbs already controlled Prizren. Besides this, Serbian Crown Prince Alexander was seen as a successful leader because his armies had no trouble taking over Macedonia and Kosovo. On the other hand, Crown Prince Danilo failed in commanding his armies and displayed an obvious lack of military talents. This meant that the unification of the Serbian lands under the Petrovic-Njegos dynasty was highly unlikely.

The Greek Efforts

Greek flagship Georgios Averof, *the most modern vessel used during the First Balkan War*
https://en.wikipedia.org/wiki/First_Balkan_War#/media/File:Greek_c ruiser_Georgios_Averof_in_1909.jpg

Greece had two armies in the field during the First Balkan War. The Army of Thessaly was the main force, and it was under the command of Crown Prince Constantine (later ruled as King Constantine I of Greece). Its main goal was to occupy Thessaly and its city of Thessaloniki. It was of paramount importance to achieve this before the Bulgarians arrived since Greece had no territorial agreement with its allies. The Greek chief command wanted this army to advance all the way to Bitola and take over southern Macedonia in the process. The second Greek force was the Army of Epirus, which was under the command of General Konstantinos Sapountzakis. Its main task was to take the Albanian city of Ioannina.

The Ottoman army in Thessaly consisted of the 8th Corps, which had three divisions, a brigade, and a cavalry. In total, they numbered around forty thousand men. Their commander was Hasan Tahsin Pasha. Aside from the 8th Corps, the Ottomans also had eighteen thousand infantry soldiers stationed at Epirus. They were reinforced by the local Albanian population, which was loyal to the empire. Hasan Tahsin Pasha was aware that he was outnumbered and didn't want to risk losing his men in an offensive, so he chose to use his whole army to set up a defensive strategy.

Thessaly

Greece declared war on the Ottoman Empire on October 18th, and on the same day, the Army of Thessaly crossed the border. It was divided into two columns, with one advancing to the towns of Elassona and Servia. The other column went in the direction of Petra. The Ottomans were in control of the Meluna mountain pass that the Greek army needed to cross, but they did nothing to contest the enemy. They anticipated the attack and instead chose to wait just northwest of Elassona.

The first clash of the Greek and Ottoman forces occurred on October 9th in the Battle of Sarantaporo. The Sarantaporo pass was one of the Ottomans' major defensive points because it controlled the entrance point to Macedonia. The battle lasted for only one day, and the Greeks won an overwhelming victory. They used a full-frontal attack, which broke the Ottoman defense. The Greeks suffered 187 dead, while the Turks had around 700. The Turks were forced to retreat northward, and in their haste, they left behind all of their military equipment. The Greeks didn't follow immediately. Their troops were unaccustomed to the rough mountainous terrain, and they had difficulties continuing forward since they were overwhelmed with exhaustion. Thus, they failed to strike a decisive blow to the Ottomans.

Another major battle, the Battle of Yenidje, started on October 20th and lasted until November 2nd. This time, the Ottomans were reinforced by troops from Bitola, and they were able to hold off the Greek advance. But the very next day, the Greek forces launched another full-frontal attack and overran the Turkish defense line. Because of the swampy ground that surrounded Yenidje, the Greeks were not able to establish their artillery, so their infantry charged without protection. Their success had a high price, as over 1,200 Greek soldiers died or were wounded. Still, the Ottoman losses were greater, with around two thousand lost lives and wounded soldiers.

The Greek army was now able to turn east and march toward their main goal of Thessaloniki. The Ottomans destroyed the bridge that would take the Greek army across the Vardar River, but there was still a railroad bridge in use. This one wasn't destroyed because the Turks needed it to transport their supplies in Macedonia.

Before reaching Thessaloniki, a brief fight took place at Servia. After the battle, the Greeks were afraid the Ottomans would attack their left flank, so they dispatched the 5th Division under the command of Colonel Mathiopulos to the north toward Florina. This not only ensured the protection of their left flank but also gave the Greeks a foothold in Macedonia. From Florina, it was possible to dispatch a force to Bitola and claim at least part of Macedonia for Greece. But the Ottomans still had Vardar Army forces stationed in southern Macedonia. They met the advance of the Greek 5th Division and defeated it in a small battle at Klidion. Now, the Greeks were forced to retreat and regroup southward.

The main Greek army, which was under the command of the Crown Prince Constantine, marched to Thessaloniki but only after he heard that the Bulgarian army was on its way. He couldn't allow his allies to occupy the city before the Greeks. Tahsin Pasha decided not to defend Thessaloniki and peacefully turned it over to the crown prince. Although Constantine sent a message to the leader of the Bulgarian army, Georgi Todorov, to divert his forces and join the Thracian front, the Bulgarians arrived in Thessaloniki. Todorov demanded the city be split between Greece and Bulgaria. Crown Prince Constantine would not have any of this, and he allowed the Bulgarian army a short rest in the city before sending them on their way. Although Thessaloniki and the whole region of Thessaly became part of Greece, it remained a point of interest for the Bulgarians, and it would contribute to the beginning of the Second Balkan War.

But while the Greeks and Bulgarians quarreled about the city, the Ottomans took the opportunity to retreat and reinforce their position in Bitola, where the Serbian Army was struggling. The Greeks also decided to remain in Thessaloniki instead of marching to Bitola, where they could have prevented the fleeing Ottomans from concentrating their forces in Albania. The Greeks' hesitation would cost them precious time and men in Epirus.

The Ottomans had the opportunity to exploit the rivalry between the Greeks and the Bulgarians, and perhaps they would have been able to defend the city if they chose to take advantage of the tensions between the two nations. Instead, Tahsin Pasha decided to retreat to Macedonia, where the Ottomans still had a significant force.

Epirus

Even before Greece officially declared war on the Ottoman Empire, they sent two of their vessels to the Preveza harbor and used torpedoes on two Turkish battleships, rendering them useless. On October 18th, the army stationed in Epirus crossed into Ottoman territory at Arta and slowly advanced to the northwest, occupying the town of Filippiada by October 26th. At this town, Commander Constantine Zapundsakis divided the Epirus army into two columns. One was sent farther north, while the second column advanced through the Gulf of Arta, where it encountered heavy Ottoman resistance. On November 2nd, the Greek army started the siege of Preveza, and in just two days, it managed to take it. Preveza was a strategically important city because it allowed the Greeks to advance through Epirus from the sea.

The Ottomans were much more determined to defend their position in Epirus than in Thessaly, and their commander, Esad Pasha, mounted a significant resistance against the Greek advance. The Ottoman army, as well as the rough terrain of the Epirus region, significantly slowed the movement of the Greek forces. After the siege of Preveza, foreign volunteers joined the Greeks and reinforced their army with a corps under the command of Italian General Ricciotti Garibaldi (a son of Giuseppe Garibaldi, a famous Italian general who contributed to the foundation of the Kingdom of Italy in 1861). The Greek army and the foreign volunteers marched to Ioannina, which was an Ottoman fortification in Epirus that was as important as Scutari was in Albania. Ioannina was also the capital of the wider administrative region of Ioannina Vilayet. The city itself had a Greek population, but the majority of the population of the whole vilayet was Albanian. In Ioannina, the Ottomans modernized the fortification and mounted ninety big guns on its walls. The fortification was also surrounded by barbed wire, trenches, and bunkers. Since the city was located on the shore of a lake, a small fort was also built on an island northeast of the city. The garrison in Ioannina was reinforced by the troops fleeing Bitola.

Because of the position and the defense of the city, the Greeks were unable to besiege and completely cut it off. The city would always remain open toward the Albanian hinterlands, from where it could acquire supplies since the local Albanian population supported the Ottomans.

In November, the Greeks surrounded the city, but they were forced to leave it open to the north, as it was impossible to approach that area due to heavy defenses. The Greek army was reinforced in November, not only by the foreign volunteers but also by the 2nd

Division of the Army of Thessaly. However, by December, the twenty-five thousand Greek soldiers who arrived at Ioannina were facing an Ottoman force thirty-five thousand strong. The Greek artillery was stationed to the south of the city since this position would give them the most effectiveness. Nevertheless, the artillery failed to damage the city walls enough for the infantry attack. By mid-December, the Greeks realized they were unable to conquer Ioannina, but unlike their allies, they didn't sign the December armistice. The Greek efforts at Ioannina continued uninterrupted.

The Sea War

The main task of the Greek army in the First Balkan War was to use the navy to block the mouth of the Dardanelles and the coast of Asia Minor. They had to do this to prevent the Ottomans from supplying their European army with more men and military equipment. But in order to achieve an effective blockade, the Greek navy had to occupy some of the Ottoman-controlled islands in the Aegean Sea. Tenedos was seized on October 20th. Seven days later, the island of Lemnos was under Greek control. This also effectively closed the Dardanelles, but the Greeks continued and took Imbros, Thassos, and Samothrace. Luckily, the islands didn't prepare much resistance. The Greek navy also had to patrol the waters around Smyrna to prevent any of the Ottoman ships from leaving the harbor.

After easily capturing the islands in the north Aegean, the Greeks focused their attention on some of the southern islands under Ottoman rule. Psara, Chios, Lesbos, and Tenedos (Turkish Bozcaada) were all captured by November 27th. It took more time for the Greeks to take over these islands because the Ottomans prepared a defense. The fighting in Chios and the main port of Lesbos, Mytilene, lasted until late December and early January. The Greek navy also avoided occupying Samos because it was already under Italian occupation. However, in March 1913, the Greek navy landed there too.

The largest naval battle occurred on December 16ᵗʰ at the mouth of the Dardanelles. It is known as the Battle of Elli. The battle started with the Ottoman warships *Barbaros Hayrettin* and *Mecidiye* exiting the strait to break the Greek blockade of the Dardanelles. The ships had the support of the artillery, which fired from the Ottoman forts on the mainland, both on the European and Asian sides of the strait. The initial attack lasted only for one hour, and both sides suffered heavy losses. The Ottomans were quickly forced to retreat. Two days later, the Turkish attempted another breakthrough and failed again. However, the Greeks were only able to declare a victory in the Dardanelles in January. This victory brought them complete control over the Aegean Sea.

The Greek navy didn't only fight in the Aegean Sea. It was also active in the Adriatic and Ionian Seas. There, they attacked and blocked the Ottoman port of Vlore in Albania. They blocked the whole Albanian coast from December 3ʳᵈ until February 27ᵗʰ. That means that the provisional government of Vlore was continuously blocked and unable to coordinate its actions with the capital in Anatolia.

The Ottoman fleet did have one major success; it helped maintain the defensive line at Chataldja. Another success was the Ottoman light cruiser *Hamidiye*, which managed to break out of Dardanelles on December 22ⁿᵈ. The *Hamidiye* continued to cruise the Mediterranean waters without being detected, and it was the only reliable Ottoman vessel that had access to many ports. The Greeks attempted to find and sink the *Hamidiye* throughout the war, but they were unsuccessful. The *Hamidiye*'s voyage also served to boost the morale of the Ottoman forces, as the men listened to the tales of its epic journey and its ability to elude the Greek navy. The Ottomans truly had little else to celebrate, so the *Hamidiye* was regarded as a light in the dark of the war.

In the Black Sea, the small Bulgarian navy managed to defeat the Ottomans. It is even believed that the Bulgarians scored a hit on the *Hamidiye* when it showed up near Varna on November 21st. However, that one hit wasn't enough to stop the little cruiser. Although the vessel suffered some damage, and some of its crew was lost, the *Hamidiye* safely reached Constantinople, where it could be repaired and resupplied for future actions in the Aegean Sea. But for the Bulgarian navy, the fact that they chased the *Hamidiye* away was a great victory. They could not afford to be cut off from Russia on the Black Sea, as that was their greatest ally.

Chapter 5 – The Armistice

Delegates of the Balkan States that took part in the London Conference
https://en.wikipedia.org/wiki/London_Conference_of_1912%E2%80%931913#/media/File:Potpisnici_londonskog_mira.jpg

When the defensive line at Chataldja couldn't be broken, Tsar Ferdinand of Bulgaria changed his political stance and started advocating for peace talks. Thus, the negotiations for an armistice started on November 25th, 1912, and it took five sessions for it to be concluded on December 3rd.

At Chataldja, the Bulgarian and Ottoman armies remained in position while the negotiations were in process. When the peace talks started, the Ottoman Empire was already significantly reduced, with its territories in Europe being occupied by Bulgarian and Serbian forces. The only remaining Ottoman territories in Europe were a small portion of Eastern Thrace, the Gallipoli Peninsula, and the besieged cities of Scutari, Ioannina, and Adrianople. The Bulgarians pushed for peace talks due to the inability of the allied armies to take over these cities and break the defense of Chataldja.

But before any peace talks could be established, a ceasefire was needed. The Bulgarians sent the president of their parliament, Stoyan Danev, and General Mihail Savov to represent not only their own country but also the interests of Serbia and Montenegro. Greece sent Dimitrios Panas, their ambassador in Sofia. The Ottoman Empire chose Nazim Pasha as its main representative.

The Balkan allies demanded that the Ottomans abandon all their European territories west of Chataldja, but the Ottomans couldn't agree to this. The armistice also demanded that the three fortresses that were under siege would not receive any new provisions and that the armies were to stay in their positions while the peace talks took place. The Ottomans also had to lift the blockade of the Black Sea and allow the Bulgarians to have uninterrupted trade and communication with Russia. In addition, they had to allow the Bulgarians to use the railroad past Adrianople so they could resupply their troops at Chataldja. Greece refused to sign the armistice because they wouldn't gain Ioannina, so the siege of the Ioannina fortress continued.

In general, the terms of the armistice favored the Balkan allies. It would give all of the military objectives to the Serbs, and the Bulgarians would receive permission to send supplies and equipment to reinforce their troops in the field. But Bulgaria, Greece, and Montenegro still had to fight to get the fortresses they needed, as the Ottomans were determined to retain Ioannina, Scutari, and

Adrianople. The Bulgarians hoped they could use the time the negotiations gave them to take Adrianople by surprise, but that would break the armistice and jeopardize the peace talks. If they gave up on this city, the Ottoman Empire would accept peace then and there. But since the Bulgarians were aware they would not get the whole of Macedonia due to the Serbian presence, they wanted compensation in Thrace, making Adrianople a perfect choice.

The London Peace Conference

While the armistice was being negotiated at Chataldja, representatives of the Balkan League and the Ottoman Empire were sent to London to start negotiating peace. The first conference they attended took place on December 16th, 1912, at St. James's Palace. Stoyan Danev abandoned the armistice talks in Chataldja to attend the London Conference as the representative of Bulgaria. The Greeks sent their prime minister, Eleftherios Venizelos, while the Montenegrins sent former Prime Minister Lazar Mijuskovic. Serbia was represented by former Prime Minister Stojan Novakovic. The Ottomans sent their ambassador in France, Mustafa Reshid Pasha, to London.

The Ottomans immediately started delaying the peace talks in hopes that they would have enough time to reinforce their armies and mount defenses of the besieged cities. They also hoped that the allies would give in to the ever-present discord among themselves, especially over the issue of Macedonia. The Ottomans managed to delay the talks by stating that Greece did not have the right to be a part of the peace since they didn't sign the armistice. They eventually conceded, and the negotiations began on December 24th.

But as soon as the talks started, they were again delayed, this time over the issue of Adrianople and some islands at the mouth of the Dardanelles. The Ottomans would not cede these territories to Bulgaria and Greece because they regarded them as being vital for the defense of their capital, Constantinople. Finally, on January 1st, 1913, the Ottoman Empire proposed they would accept the loss of all territories west of Adrianople, but it would not give away the city itself or the rest of Thrace, nor would it allow any of the islands to be taken by Greece. This was unacceptable to the Balkan League, and the peace negotiations came to a halt once again. Five days later, the peace talks were suspended.

The second conference in London gathered the ambassadors of the six Great European Powers (Germany, the UK, France, Austro-Hungary, Italy, and Russia), the signatories of the Treaty of Berlin. Because the Balkan nations and the Ottoman Empire were unable to reach an agreement, the representatives of the Great Powers decided to meet. The representatives of the Balkan League and the Ottoman Empire were not present at this conference, and it became clear to them that the settlement of the First Balkan War would happen without them. The Great Powers were concerned that the First Balkan War would grow into a larger European war, mainly because Austria-Hungary refused to stand by and observe the growing power of its new neighbor, Serbia. The Habsburgs already launched some military actions in Bosnia and Herzegovina, as well as in Galicia (where Russia started stirring problems). This London conference failed to prevent this great European war from occurring, but they managed to postpone the Great War until 1914.

The leader of the London Conference was Sir Edward Grey, the secretary of foreign affairs in the United Kingdom. The main goal of the conference was to oversee the peace talks of the Balkan nations, as well as to protect the interests the Great Powers had in the Balkans, especially Austria-Hungary, Russia, and Italy. They wanted to replace the Treaty of Berlin with a new one, which would accommodate the new situation in the Balkan Peninsula. To achieve this, the ambassadors had to agree on what would happen to the Aegean Islands and a new border in Thrace, which would separate Bulgaria and the Ottoman Empire.

The conference also had to deal with the national question of the Albanians. They had proclaimed independence on November 28th, 1912, and established a provisional government under the leadership of Ismail Kemal Bey. The Albanian presence in the Balkans can be traced to the medieval period, but they never had an independent state before, only a principality headed by the local nobility, which was ruled over by Greece or Serbia. For a long time, the Albanians had been under Ottoman rule, but since it had nearly collapsed, the Albanians were forced to act.

The Serbian Army slowly progressed through the territory that is today central Albania. There, they took over the port city of Durres. This was a vital commercial port, and the Albanians couldn't allow the Serbs to occupy such an important city in the middle of their newly independent state. The Albanians were not the only ones bothered by the Serbian presence on the Adriatic Sea. The Italians wanted to keep their predominance of the Strait of Otranto and the mouth of the Adriatic. The Habsburgs were extremely antagonized when Serbia gained access to the sea. They didn't want their immediate neighbor to grow in power and become a regional leader. They also thought that Russia was using Serbia in order to keep Austro-Hungarian ambitions in the Balkans in check. Since the Habsburgs had lost Italy, their only exit to the sea was through what is today Croatia. They couldn't allow a third strong state to appear on the Adriatic, which was why Austria-Hungary needed to create an Albanian state. It would be a new ethnic state under the control of the Habsburgs.

Since the Austro-Hungarians weren't in conflict with Greece, they didn't care about the southern borders of the newly created state of Albania. To them, the important thing was to cut off Serbia by expanding the northern Albanian border to include Scutari, Gjakova, and Prizren. However, the Greeks didn't have any of the Great Powers as an ally. The Greek navy blocked the Albanian provisional government at Vlore, and the Great Powers promised Greece could take Ioannina if they could conquer it in turn for the release of Vlore.

But the southern borders of Albania were not yet resolved simply because the Great Powers had no direct interest in these territories. On December 20th, 1912, an independent Albanian state was recognized by the ambassadors of the Great Powers seated at the London Conference. There was nothing Serbia could do to keep its portion of the Adriatic Sea.

The Bulgarian-Greek Dispute

The allies of the Balkan League started showing signs of discord even before the signing of the December armistice. The first problems arose between the Bulgarians and Greeks and the race for Thessaloniki. The Greeks entered the city first, but the Bulgarians arrived a day after and claimed that the city should be divided. While both armies were stationed in the city, the Greek prime minister proposed that Bulgaria should share southern Macedonia. Thessaloniki, Serres, and Kavala would go to Greece, allowing it to have a common border with Serbia. However, the Bulgarians wanted to occupy the majority of Macedonia, claiming that they had the right to do so because their army and involvement in the war was greater.

The dispute between Greece and Bulgaria wasn't resolved with the signing of the armistice. Even after the victories their armies had achieved, neither side showed goodwill or any intention to resolve the dispute. Instead, they left it to the Great Powers. The representatives of Greece and Bulgaria met in London on three occasions to discuss the dispute. Greek Prime Minister Venizelos made a new proposal to the Bulgarian representative, Danev, in which Greece would give up the claim of much of southern Macedonia but keep Thessaloniki. Danev responded that it was not up to him to make such decisions. He was confident in the strength of the Bulgarian army and advised the government in Sofia that they should fight Greece and claim the city for Bulgaria.

Unfortunately, the Bulgarians failed to resolve their dispute with Greece in London. Modern scholars believe that Danev should have accepted Greece's proposal, as it would have put Bulgaria in a much better position to negotiate the issue of Macedonia with Serbia. Macedonia was their main goal anyway, not Thessaloniki.

The Bulgarian-Serbian Dispute

Because Serbia lost its approach to the Adriatic Sea, it wanted compensation for the lost territories, so the Serbian leaders turned to Macedonia. After all, they regarded Macedonia as a part of Serbia's cultural legacy, and they never really planned to concede much of the territory to Bulgaria, as was predicted by the March 1912 treaty. In fact, many of the government leaders, as well as the members of the paramilitary organization called the Black Hand, opposed any arbitration with Bulgaria. The loss of northern Albania only made the Serbians determined to gain territory in Macedonia, even if it meant a conflict with their ally Bulgaria.

Even before the Albanian state was recognized by the Great Powers in London, the Serbians started consolidating their military power in occupied Macedonia. The Bulgarian leaders in Sofia were aware of this because early on, Serbians started arresting any Bulgarian administrators and closing the Bulgarian schools in the area. Bulgaria relied on Russia to resolve the issue of Macedonia with Serbia, but Russia failed to support Bulgarian interests, even though it accepted the role of arbitrator in the treaty of March 1912.

Bulgaria remained determined to keep most of Macedonia, and it refused to accept that Serbia should get compensation for their advance in the Adriatic at their expense. On January 13th, 1913, the Serbian government filed a formal request for the revision of the March 1912 treaty. They claimed that Bulgaria had conquered more territory in Thrace than was planned, and since Serbia lost its gains in Albania, it should be compensated. They also mentioned that the Bulgarians failed to send troops to the Vardar front; the Serbian Army had sent troops to Adrianople when their Bulgarian allies needed help. The Bulgarian government didn't respond to the Serbian request, as they still hoped Russia would intervene. What they didn't consider was that the absence of the Bulgarian troops in Macedonia made the March 1912 treaty legally irrelevant. The Serbs occupied most of Macedonia, and by international law, they had the right to ignore the agreement that had been made before the war.

The Bulgarian-Romanian Dispute

The Bulgarian government had yet another problem to deal with after the London Conference, as their defeat over the Ottomans changed the power balance in the Balkan Peninsula. The Romanians were never completely a part of the Ottoman Empire, so they regarded themselves as the single strongest power that should act as the gendarme in the region. Because Romania was an Austro-Hungarian ally and friendly toward the Ottoman Empire, Bulgaria needed to ensure it would not meddle once the war broke out. They couldn't leave their rear open to Romania without knowing its intentions. So, Sofia reached out to Bucharest on the eve before the declaration of war on the Ottoman Empire in hopes they could reach some agreement. The Romanian prime minister, Titu Maiorescu, refused to give a decisive answer. He wanted to wait and see the outcome of the war before making any decisions that would influence the future of his country.

Once it became clear that Bulgaria was winning the war and once Romania saw Bulgaria's gains in Thrace, the Romanian government approached Sofia with the demand for compensation at the expense of the northeastern Bulgarian territories. They were after the increasingly important Danube port of Silistra. But by January 1913, the Romanians expanded their demands and requested that Bulgaria turn over Dobrogea, a fertile corner of northwestern Bulgaria. The Treaty of Berlin had previously divided this territory between Bulgaria and Romania, but now Romania wanted it all. Romania wanted complete control of the south bank of the Danube Delta, as well as the fertile land that would feed Bucharest. In fact, Romania considered the military occupation of the southern Bulgarian part of Dobruja, but Austria-Hungary assured the Romanian leaders they would eventually gain the disputed territory without military intervention.

To the Bulgarians, Romania's request of southern Dobruja seemed like blackmail. They were reluctant to give up any territory while the Bulgarian army was conquering and adding to the greatness of the state. However, not wanting to expose themselves to another potential enemy, the Bulgarian leaders avoided giving an ultimate answer to the Romanian request. Instead, they offered minimal border adjustments and the possibility for further negotiations. But this tactic only served to buy them some time. At the end of February, the Bulgarian forces at Adrianople were fighting again, and the Great Powers put pressure on Bulgaria to cede some territory. Bulgaria was reluctant to part from Macedonia or its gains in Thrace, but it finally agreed to resolve the dispute with Romania. The conference where the delegates would meet was organized in St. Petersburg on February 24th, 1913. Because Russia agreed to host the conference, the Bulgarians took it as a sign that their greatest ally would help them resolve the Macedonian issue. The Bulgarian faith in Russia during the First Balkan War was largely misplaced, though.

Bulgarian diplomacy failed when its leaders refused to cede the ethnically Bulgarian part of Dobruja to Romania. Many of the state leaders, as well as Tsar Ferdinand, wanted to cede this territory and secure the northern border with Romania, as they were aware of the rising problem with Serbia over the territory in Macedonia. But Bulgaria relied on Russia for protection against military advances Bucharest might launch against them. Because they refused to cede Dobruja, the Bulgarians would pay the price in Macedonia, where the loss of their territory would be greater than anticipated.

The Ottoman Empire during the Armistice

The Young Turks took the opportunity of the armistice to seize power in Constantinople again. They were led by Enver Bey, and they managed to overthrow the government on January 23rd, 1913. They thought that Grand Vizier Kamil Pasha was preparing to surrender

Adrianople to Bulgaria, and they used this propaganda as their main motivation. The Young Turks didn't want to sign a peace treaty; they intended to continue the war, save Adrianople, and regain at least some of the lost territories. Kamil Pasha was forced to resign since his life was threatened. The minister of war, Nazim Pasha, was shot and killed because the Young Turks blamed him for the Ottoman Empire's military failures.

The former minister of war, Mahmud Shevket Pasha, became the new grand vizier, and the new government tasked him with retaining Adrianople by any means possible. In London, the Young Turks made a new proposal to the ambassadors of the Great Powers. They wanted to divide Adrianople in such a way that the part of the city that lies on the right bank of the Maritsa River would belong to Bulgaria. The Young Turks would also agree to give up their claims over the islands in the Aegean Sea and leave their disposition to the Great Powers. The Bulgarians were not able to accept this agreement due to the accumulating problems they had with all of their allies and neighbors. Other members of the Balkan League also rejected this proposal since they would rather resume the war. And on February 3rd, 1913, the war continued.

Chapter 6 – The War Continues

The Ottomans surrender their flag to Montenegrin King Nikola in Scutari
https://upload.wikimedia.org/wikipedia/commons/5/53/Skadar_predaj a_zastave.jpg

On January 30th, 1913, all of the allies denounced the armistice. The fighting resumed on February 3rd, with five locations becoming war fronts. In the Albanian territories, at Scutari and Ioannina, the fighting never really stopped. But after the denunciation of the armistice, the fighting at Adrianople, Gallipoli, and the line at Chataldja resumed. The Ottomans used the break in the fighting to reinforce their troops and resupply Adrianople and Chataldja. However, the Bulgarians failed to do the same. Since the autumn of 1912, the Bulgarian forces at Chataldja had very low morale, and it remained so after the armistice ended. The Montenegrins besieging Scutari had spent their supplies, and the lack of food and military equipment took a toll on their morale. The Greeks who besieged Ioannina didn't even have an opportunity to experience any serious fighting. The Serbian Army was the only one that achieved all of its goals since all of the Ottomans left Kosovo and Macedonia. The Serbs were ready to help their allies and dispatch troops to the front.

The Gallipoli Front

The Ottoman Empire's new government decided to make a bold move and try to relieve the pressure on Adrianople by launching an attack in the Gallipoli Peninsula and Şarköy, a city on the banks of the Sea of Marmara. They did so on February 7th, 1913, but they were aware this was just one of the many efforts they would have to endure to relieve the city. The plan was devised by Enver Bey, who was only a chief of staff at the moment. In 1914, he would lead the Ottoman forces into the Great War as a pasha (a title of a high-ranking man).

At Gallipoli, the Bulgarians had a newly organized 4th Army, which included the 7th Rila Division, under the command of General Stiliyan Kovachev. The army counted 92,289 officers and their men. The army's main purpose was to defend the Bulgarian position at Gallipoli, as it guarded the rear of the Bulgarian siege of Adrianople and Chataldja. The Ottomans started their attack at the town of Bulair on January 26th, but the Bulgarians were ready. The 7th Rila Division, which was under the command of General Georgi Todorov, took a position along the defensive line, which was as wide as the Gallipoli Peninsula (around 4.5 miles).

The Ottomans intended to break this Bulgarian defensive line, clear the peninsula of the enemy, and retreat to Şarköy, where they would meet up with their comrades at the Sea of Marmara. The Bulgarians were outnumbered, as the Ottoman forces included the 27th Division and the Myureteb Division, which together counted around fifty thousand men. The 7th Rila Division had only ten thousand men. However, the Bulgarians had seventy-eight guns mounted along their defensive line, which gave them an advantage over the Ottomans' thirty-six guns.

The Battle of Bulair started on the morning of February 8th, 1913, with the appearance of an Ottoman cruiser, the *Mecidiye*, which supported the advance of the infantry by firing on Bulgarian defenses from the sea. The Ottoman soldiers launched an attack on the Bulgarian left flank, which was stationed next to the shores of the Sea of Marmara. Soon after, the Turkish soldiers attacked the right flank of the Bulgarian army, as this position quickly ran out of ammunition and was open to an attack.

However, in the center of the peninsula, the Bulgarians managed to hold their position, even though they suffered constant artillery fire. They were desperate, but they held on. The advancing Ottoman forces entered the mist and smoke caused by the dampness and gunfire, and they became disoriented, allowing the Bulgarians to launch a counterattack. In the early afternoon, the Ottoman forces were retreating, and the Bulgarian army pursued them. By the evening, both sides found themselves in the same positions as before the battle. The Ottomans realized they had lost many soldiers; there were more than six thousand dead and eighteen thousand wounded or lost. The Bulgarian had much lower casualties, with only 114 dead and 416 wounded.

In the meantime, the Ottomans launched their second phase of the attack at Şarköy, a port in the Sea of Marmara. The attack started on February 7th when Ottoman battleships started bombarding the Bulgarian troops stationed there. The Bulgarians had no other choice but to retreat two miles away from the shore, where they mounted their artillery and started bombarding the Ottomans. West of Şarköy, the Ottoman 10th Corps, which had around forty thousand men, landed and moved toward the port city. This infantry attack presented the Bulgarians with much difficulty because if the Ottomans reached the northern shore of the Sea of Marmara and established their garrison there, they would be a threat to the rear of the Bulgarian Thracian army stationed at Chataldja. The Bulgarians had to stop the Ottomans from continuing the landing, and the fighting lasted for the next three days. The Bulgarians had to use airplane support to stop the Turkish advance.

The Ottomans gave up on Şarköy and decided to use their naval power to reinforce their troops at Gallipoli. But even there, the Turkish navy failed to establish a strong presence and was unable to cut off the Bulgarian army at Gallipoli. Instead of focusing on Gallipoli, the Ottomans decided to launch an attack on the Bulgarian 1st Army, which was positioned at the southern part of the Chataldja defensive line. This attack also started on February 7th and forced the Bulgarian army to retreat around twenty kilometers (twelve miles) back and assume the second defensive line. The Bulgarians only did so to avoid exposing their rear to the Ottomans, and at the second defensive line, they were able to easily divert the attack.

In Eastern Thrace, the Ottomans undertook an aggressive offensive. They hoped it would relieve Adrianople of the pressure it felt and maybe even end the siege. Their attack was bold and brave, but the Ottoman army lacked command and training. No matter how much of a fighting spirit the Young Turks had, they simply didn't have a modern 20th-century army at their disposal. The lack of able officers who would lead the armies was apparent, especially in the failure to coordinate the attacks at Gallipoli with the landing at Şarköy. But these battles in Gallipoli and Chataldja provided the Ottomans with much-needed experience, and the defenses they would mount here during the Great War would prove to be much more successful.

The Bulgarians who fought in the Gallipoli Peninsula and the northern shores of the Sea of Marmara were frightened by the Ottomans' resolve and strong attacks. But they didn't give in to panic. Instead, they bravely held their positions and used their military advantage wisely. These were the most successful defensive battles of the Bulgarian army in the Balkan Wars. They held so well that the

Ottoman forces were exhausted and could no longer plan another offensive. This meant that the Bulgarians gained the initiative in the war, and although they were outnumbered, they would use this initiative to bring about the fall of Adrianople in March 1913.

The Siege of Ioannina

The Greeks never signed the armistice with the Ottomans, so their efforts in Epirus continued without interruptions. However, this remote and hostile region proved to be very difficult for the Greek army. The winter came, and the mountainous region in which the soldiers were stationed became even more hostile. Many Greeks lost their lives due to exposure to cold and the lack of food. And as if these troubles were not enough, the Greeks lacked the manpower to completely besiege Ioannina.

Still, they were resolved to take the fortified city before any peace was concluded. Because of this, Greek military leaders decided to transfer three divisions of the Army of Thessaly to Epirus. By January, the Greeks surrounding Ioannina numbered around twenty-eight thousand men, and they were supported by eight artillery pieces and six airplanes. Although everything was peaceful in Thessaly, their dispute with the Bulgarians around Macedonia prevented them from transferring even more troops to Ioannina. They needed to leave a part of their force in Thessaloniki and guard the city against their allies.

The Ottoman defenders within the city walls didn't have better conditions than their enemies at the gates. Most of the civilians in Ioannina were ethnic Greeks, so the Ottoman army couldn't rely on their loyalty. Since the Greeks failed to surround the city, the deserters were left with a secure way out. Some of the civilians helped the Turkish army because they hoped that the Ottoman Empire would support an independent Albania or at least an autonomous province, with Ioannina as its new capital. Ioannina was protected to the northeast by the Ottoman 6th Corps at Korçë, where they established a presence after they were chased out of Macedonia. But on December 20th, the Greeks managed to push the Ottoman 6th Corps out of Korçë and establish Greek control over the northeastern approach to Ioannina. This meant that the flow of food, military supplies, and men into Ioannina slowed down.

The fighting at Ioannina intensified during the last days of 1912. Artillery exchanged fire almost every day. It seems that the defenders of Ioannina didn't lack any ammunition since they continuously bombed the Greek positions around the city. However, they were ineffective, as their guns would rarely hit their target. But the main fortification of Ioannina, the Bizani fortress, resisted all Greek attempts to take it, even when Greek airplanes dropped hand grenades from the air. The Albanian irregulars constantly harassed the Greeks in Epirus with guerilla-style attacks. On January 12th, 1913, the Albanians destroyed the facilities in the port of Santi Quaranta (Sarande), the main port Greece used to supply its army that was besieging Ioannina.

The Greeks decided to launch a large-scale attack on January 20th. They were successful in overrunning the flank fortifications, but the Bizani fortress remained unconquered. The attack on this central fort led to the Greeks having many casualties (over 1,200 dead), which prompted them to end their attacks. However, if the Greeks had persisted, the attack likely would have succeeded. The Ottoman leaders later admitted that Ioannina would have been breached if the enemy soldiers pressed their attack at least until the evening.

The Greeks were running out of time. Their main goal was to take Ioannina before the peace was concluded in London. Their representative's efforts to achieve an agreement with Bulgaria at the peace conference came to a halt. But the London Ambassador Conference was making progress and already deciding what would be the borders of the new Albanian state. The Greek leaders were afraid that if Ioannina withstood the siege, the ambassadors would include it in the independent Albanian state.

General Konstantinos Sapountzakis was relieved of his command after the failure on January 20th, and the command over the Army of Epirus was given to Crown Prince Constantine. He planned the final attack, which would begin on March 4th. His strategy was to use the right flank to engage the enemy, making them think that was the main attack, while the left flank pushed forward and breached the city. During the attack, the Greeks used artillery to bring the fortress of Bizani down. The fighting took place between March 4th and 6th March, and it ended when the Greek forces managed to overwhelm their Ottoman enemy. Esad Pasha surrendered Ioannina unconditionally. The Greeks took around thirty-three prisoners of war and confiscated all of the Ottoman military equipment they found in the city. Ioannina was the first of the three besieged cities to fall, and it was also the greatest accomplishment of the Greek forces during the Balkan Wars.

The Siege of Adrianople

During the armistice, all fighting at Adrianople stopped. However, the Ottomans were unable to resupply the city, especially because the conditions of the armistice dictated them not to attempt it. This ensured that, by winter, the city would run out of food and military supplies. But the Ottomans still had one hope. They could use their forces at Chataldja or Gallipoli to launch an offensive that would relieve the city. However, the Ottoman garrison within the city couldn't rely on this. Instead, they started improving their fortifications, planted mines, installed floodlights, and established a secure radio connection with Constantinople. The hopes of the Adrianople soldiers were reinforced when the Young Turks' coup happened, as the new government promised it would not give up on the city. But the winter was already there, and the conditions for an Ottoman attack were not good.

The Bulgarian army was not eager to fight either. They were aware that of all the fronts, their army had the best possibility to succeed at Adrianople. The Bulgarian generals Savov and Fichev didn't want to risk high casualties, especially after losing so many soldiers at the Battle of Chataldja. The Bulgarian army also wasn't prepared for the long siege of the city, as they lacked the technical material for the continuous attack on the city's forts. Savov hoped that the Ottomans' inability to resupply the city would be enough for Adrianople to surrender during the cold months of winter. He was reluctant to use an open infantry attack since he was sure the Ottomans would gun his soldiers down. Instead, Savov approached his allies, the Serbs, asking for heavy artillery that would ensure a Bulgarian victory and protect the infantry. On February 13th, the Serbs arrived with heavy artillery, but they conditioned its use, specifying that they would ask for compensation at a later date. The Bulgarians agreed, making it clear they accepted to compensate the Serbian Army, albeit only financially.

The bombardment of Adrianople continued as soon as the armistice was denounced. The Bulgarians wanted to use the heavy artillery attack to raise the spirits of their soldiers and to depress those Ottomans within the city. Some of the shelling was directed toward the European quarter, as the Bulgarian leaders hoped this would make foreign ambassadors pressure the Ottomans to surrender the city. However, this tactic only demonstrated how impatient Savov was.

During the bombardment, Bulgarian military technicians worked on jamming the radio signal between Adrianople and Constantinople. This might very well be the first attempt at electronic warfare in the history of Europe. The defenders of Adrianople responded to enemy artillery fire by launching several attacks on the guns positioned nearest to the city. But they were not successful at all, and the bombardment continued uninterrupted.

The Serbian Army brought seventeen batteries and fifty-eight guns. Some of the guns were brand-new, brought to Adrianople straight from the factory. The presence of the Serbian artillery put additional pressure on the besieged city, and the Bulgarians felt as if the time was right to launch the final assault. Tsar Ferdinand, the Russian military attaché Colonel Georgi Romanovski, and the rest of the Russian general staff urged the Bulgarians to launch the attack. General Savov gave in to the pressure only when Ioannina surrendered to the Greeks. Before that, he was reluctant to order the attack because the winter had been very difficult for his army. Typhus and cholera raged among the soldiers, and the area around the city had no trees that could protect the army from snowstorms. To keep his soldiers alive, Savov had to acquire food and other supplies from Serbia.

Because of the alarming decline of the Bulgarian army's morale around Adrianople and because of the harsh winter conditions, several Bulgarian leaders strongly opposed the attack. Among them were Chief of Staff Fichev, Prime Minister Geshov, and Stoyan Danev. They told General Savov that the Bulgarian government didn't want to launch an attack because the risk of a large number of casualties was very high. However, they still wanted to conclude the siege so that they could focus on the Macedonian issue.

As you can see, Savov was under pressure, and he decided to order the attack on March 24th. He devised a plan that involved the constant bombardment of the city walls that heavily concentrated on the eastern and western sectors. The final assault would be launched on the eastern part of Adrianople. Through espionage, the Bulgarian army learned that the Turks felt unsafe in the eastern sector, and they believed that the west was heavily guarded. On top of that, the eastern sector had no river running through it that could obstruct the advance of an invading army. The Bulgarians still needed to divert the attention of the Ottoman forces at Chataldja, so they opted for a simultaneous attack on both fronts. This would prevent the Turks from sending relief armies to Adrianople.

The initial bombardment of the city surprised its defenders, and in the early morning, the infantry moved across the plains approaching the city. But the infantry attack proved to be premature. To avoid heavy losses, it had to stop at noon on the same day. Nevertheless, the bombardment continued, and under cover of night on March 25th, the Bulgarian infantry tried yet another attack. The Ottomans rushed to reinforce their southern wall because they feared that was where the main attack would come. This was a major mistake, and it is proof that the Bulgarian plan worked. The enemy never intended to breach the southern wall because that sector had only one bridge crossing the Maritsa River, which would create an opportunity for the Ottomans to quickly dispose of the Bulgarian invaders. When Mehmed Şükrü Pasha, the commander of the Ottoman Adrianople defenders, realized the main attack would come on the eastern part of the city, it was too late. He was unable to quickly dispatch his soldiers there.

The main assault on the eastern sector began on March 26th at four a.m. The Bulgarian army had immediate success there. The Ottoman army was already exhausted; they were hungry and demoralized, and they offered very little resistance. The forts in the eastern sector simply stopped resisting. Some Ottoman soldiers stationed in the forts welcomed the invaders, relieved that the siege was over. The Bulgarian cavalry entered Adrianople at nine in the morning, and they captured Şükrü Pasha, which then formally surrendered the city at one p.m.

The Serbian and Bulgarian artillery was the most important factor in the siege. They maintained the siege and made the attack possible in the first place. They also offered cover for the infantry forces to approach the city, but even before that, the constant bombardment they provided demoralized the defenders. The role of the artillery units in taking over Adrianople was noted by many military experts, who later used the same tactics during the First World War.

When the news of Adrianople's fall reached the government in Sofia, there was a lot of joy. All the Slavic nations celebrated the Bulgarian victory because the cooperation between them and the Serbs showed the world what the Slavs were capable of if they united together. Unfortunately, this victory over Adrianople would also be the last time the two armies fought together, as the discord over Macedonia was too great to ignore.

The Bulgarians had to pay a high price for the victory. As predicted, the casualties were great, with over 9,500 dead and wounded. But the Ottoman casualties were far greater, as they had fifteen thousand dead and wounded and over sixty thousand taken as prisoners of war.

General Savov ordered a simultaneous attack on Adrianople and Chataldja, where the 1ˢᵗ Bulgarian Army had the task to not only prevent the Ottomans from reinforcing their garrison in the city but also to retake the territory that had been lost in the previous months. This would allow the Bulgarians to eventually take Constantinople. But the 1ˢᵗ army was only successful in returning some of the territories, even though the fighting at Chataldja continued until April. The casualties at Chataldja were less heavy than at Adrianople, with around 450 dead.

Russia wouldn't allow the Bulgarians to advance to Constantinople. They urged their allies to stop the fighting and promised St. Petersburg would give Bulgaria full support in the peace talks. The Bulgarian government needed this reassurance, especially with the problem of Macedonia still looming over their heads. This was enough for the Bulgarian leaders to decide against pressuring their soldiers to retake Chataldja at any cost. They welcomed peace with the Ottomans because they still hoped their main prize, Macedonia, could be won.

Scutari

During the armistice, the Montenegrins continued besieging Scutari, but the fighting ceased. The Montenegrin army was poorly supplied, and they didn't have adequate shelter. Their forces were supplemented by the volunteers, mainly Montenegrins who abandoned their lives in the United States of America and the Slavs from the Habsburg Empire. Although there was no major fighting, the Montenegrins sporadically bombarded the city to probe their defenses. The Ottomans, on the other hand, used the armistice to rest and reinforce their defensive points. In December, they were bold enough to send scouts outside of the city to assess the situation and to gather food from the nearby villages that were still loyal to the Ottomans.

Hasan Riza Bey was assassinated during the armistice, and the new commander of the Ottoman forces was chosen the next day on January 31st. This man was Esad Pasha Toptani, who had previously been the second in command. He was an Albanian deputy and an opportunist. It was later discovered that he instigated the murder of Hasan Riza Bey, hoping he would gain the leadership of the new Albanian state, whether it remained within the Ottoman Empire as an autonomous entity or as an entirely independent state.

Once the armistice came to an end, King Nikola of Montenegro decided to launch a full-scale attack. The first bombardment of Scutari started on February 6th, 1913, and it was concentrated on the Bardanjolt fortress to the east of the city. The diversion was to be provided by both Montenegrin and Serbian coastal divisions to the west and south. The crown prince was to lead the Zeta Division in the main attack. They were furious, and the Montenegrins' determination finally brought them behind the barbed wire that surrounded Bardanjolt. They continued their efforts and drove the Ottomans from the fortified hill. Esad Pasha Toptani launched a counterattack, though, and managed to retake Bardanjolt. After three days of continuous fighting, the Montenegrins realized they would not take Scutari. They ended their efforts on February 9th.

Both sides suffered great losses, with the Ottomans having around 1,300 casualties and the Montenegrins and Serbs around 4,000. Another 1,500 soldiers were lost during the diversionary attack on Tarabosh, which also failed. At Brdica, the Serbian forces stopped their efforts once they saw the failure of the Zeta Division. There, the Serbian casualties amounted to 1,800 soldiers. The besiegers lacked artillery with which they could support their infantry attacks, which was the main reason the Scutari siege was a disaster. The Montenegrin political drive had persuaded the army to stay at Scutari even though they lacked the manpower and artillery needed to take the city.

King Nikola turned to the Serbians for help, just as General Savov at Adrianople had done. The Serbs responded to their ally's needs and sent thirty thousand men under the command of General Petar Bojovic. They brought seventy-two artillery pieces with them and were followed by a squadron of four airplanes. However, the terrain the Serbian Army had to traverse was so rough that the first forces only arrived at Scutari on March 18th. Because of his experience, the command over the Montenegrin and Serbian armies at Scutari was given to Serbian General Petar Bojovic, but some Montenegrins took this as a humiliation. Nevertheless, they had no choice in the matter, as they feared they would lose the support of their Serbian ally.

While the Montenegrins wanted to assume the control of Scutari by force, the ambassadors at the London Conference had different plans. Austria-Hungary advocated the new Albanian state, with Scutari as an integral part. The Russians countered this decision and sought to obtain it for Montenegro. In the end, Austria-Hungary persuaded Russia to give up Scutari. Gjakova, a town in Kosovo, would be given to Serbia in exchange.

The Great Powers proceeded to pressure the Serbian and Greek governments to stop helping the Montenegrins in their siege of Scutari. This put the Serbs in a very difficult position. The Montenegrins were not only their allies but also compatriots, and they could not abandon them in their time of need. On the other hand, the issue of Macedonia demanded the Serbs' immediate attention and allocation of resources. Their interest in Serbian Macedonia was far greater than Montenegrin Scutari.

On March 28th, the Great Powers met with the government representatives in Cetinje and then the next day in Belgrade. They demanded an immediate ceasefire and the establishment of peace talks. The Montenegrin answer to this demand was another attack on Scutari. On March 30th, they began firing on the city, and the next day, the combined army of Montenegro and Serbia launched another large-scale attack. This time, their main goal was a fortification at Tarabosh.

However, the Serbian command over the combined army didn't bring better results. They failed to breach the Ottoman defenses and were finally convinced they were unable to take the city. The Great Powers responded to this attack by sending five battleships, under the command of British Admiral Sir Cecil Burney, to the Adriatic Sea to impose a blockade on Montenegro.

The Serbian Army realized the threat the foreign fleet sailing the Adriatic Sea posed, and the Serbs decided they could no longer participate in the siege of Scutari. They started withdrawing their forces on April 10th, but they left the Serbian artillery behind so the Montenegrins could use it if they decided to continue their efforts.

The Montenegrins would not yet give up on Scutari. They decided to continue the siege despite Serbia leaving and the presence of the foreign fleet at their door. Austria-Hungary would not take this defiance, and it urged the Great Powers to land their forces and deal with the Montenegrins once and for all. However, Esad Pasha Toptani decided to surrender to Montenegro, and after some days of negotiations, he did so formally on April 22nd. It turns out the Ottomans had exhausted their defenses, and the civilians and soldiers within the city were running out of food. King Nikola decided to allow the Ottoman troops to leave the city, but he forced them to leave their artillery behind. The Montenegrins defied the Great Powers and entered Scutari on April 24th without a single shot being fired that day.

However, the conquest of the city didn't come without a price. Montenegro promised the recognition of the new Albanian state, as well as financial aid to Esad Pasha Toptani, which would help him become the leader of his country. Serbia congratulated Montenegro on its success.

After the fall of Scutari, Austria-Hungary started preparing its army for a war against Montenegro and possibly Serbia. They thought Scutari was a vital city for the survival of their puppet state of Albania, and they were ready to fight for it with or without the help of the other Great Powers. Without Albania, the Austro-Hungarian interests in the Balkans were in danger. However, before the Habsburgs could react, King Nikola realized Montenegro couldn't retain the city without facing repercussions by the Great Powers. So, on May 5th, he surrendered the city after only two weeks of holding it. The Great Powers sent a detachment nine days later to seize the city.

Chapter 7 – The Peace Before the Storm

Serbian and Greek prime ministers Nikola Pasic and Eleftherios Venizelos
https://en.wikipedia.org/wiki/Greek%E2%80%93Serbian_Alliance_of_1913#/media/File:Nikola_Pa%C5%A1i%C4%87_and_Eleftherios_Venizelos-cropped.jpeg

The First Balkan War ended when the new armistice was signed at Chataldja on April 15th, 1913. However, the last of the fighting stopped on April 22nd when Scutari surrendered to Montenegro. The end of the war wasn't the end of the efforts to reorganize the Balkan states and draw new borders. The Great Powers and the Balkan allies continued to fight for their goals, but this time, their main weapon was diplomacy. And while this was happening, the relationship between the Balkan League members deteriorated rapidly. Bulgaria was desperate, and it needed a final solution since it didn't achieve peace with the Ottoman Empire. The Bulgarian leaders lost their faith in the Russians and their promise that they would help Bulgarian interests in Macedonia. Aside from these problems, the Bulgarians also faced increasing pressure from Romania regarding Dobruja.

The first conference in which officials tried to solve the question of Dobruja was held in St. Petersburg in March 1913. This conference was secondary to the London Ambassador Conference, and its main goal was to preserve Russian interests in Bulgaria. To some extent, these interests were now being expanded to include Romania. The Russian government demanded that Romania abandon the Triple Alliance of 1882 (an alliance between Germany, Austria-Hungary, and Italy, which had the support of other European countries, among which was Romania). However, Romania resisted Russia's demands and remained loyal to its European allies. This Russian diplomatic debacle had a price, and Bulgaria had to pay it.

On May 8th, the conference in St. Petersburg decided that Bulgaria was to give the port of Silistra to Romania. Thus, the dispute between the two countries was resolved. Romania had demanded all of Dobruja, but it had to be satisfied with only Silistra. Naturally, the Bulgarians didn't like this outcome since they had always refused to cede any territory that belonged to them. The Romanians, on the other hand, continued demanding more land in southern Dobruja. But the fact that disturbed the Bulgarians the most was the realization that Russia could not guarantee the preservation of Bulgarian territory, let alone to mediate in the dispute over Macedonia.

The Alliance Between Greece and Serbia

The dispute Bulgaria had with Greece and Serbia regarding Macedonia continued to intensify throughout the early months of 1913. In regards to Greece, Bulgaria was still holding a grudge about Thessaloniki. While the Greeks were ready to give up most of the territories of southern Macedonia, including the major towns of Kavala, Serres, and Drama, they would not give up on Thessaloniki. The Bulgarians were divided on this issue. While some were ready to accept the Greek proposal, others refused to surrender even the smallest part of Macedonia. If Bulgaria had accepted the proposal constructed by Greek Prime Minister Venizelos in February 1913, they could have avoided the establishment of the Greek-Serbian alliance. They would have also been in a much better position to resist Serbian claims on Macedonia.

Bulgaria was indecisive about the Macedonian question, and during early spring, Sofia received news of a Greek army stationed in northern Macedonia launching military activities against Bulgarians. The first major clash occurred in the town of Nigrita, northeast of Thessaloniki. The Bulgarians suffered a considerable number of casualties, and it became obvious that the Greeks and Serbs had coordinated their attacks to seize Macedonia. In March, the Serbian and Greek officers met in Thessaloniki, where they paraded the streets together, wearing each other's hats as a symbol of brotherhood and alliance. By mid-March, it was apparent the war between the Serbian-Greek alliance and Bulgaria was unavoidable, but nobody dared to try to predict when it would come.

When King George I of Greece was killed on March 18th, 1913, the emotional sentiments about the dispute with Bulgaria deepened. The fate of Thessaloniki was still not decided, and new fighting broke out just outside of the city between the Greek and Bulgarian troops stationed there. Nobody ordered these attacks; they were initiated by overly emotional soldiers. The Bulgarian and Greek leaders agreed to form a joint committee to investigate these incidents and keep the peace while the matter was being resolved through diplomacy. But the commission failed to calm the situation in the city, so the hostilities between the Bulgarian and Greek forces continued.

In Macedonia, the Serbian and Greek troops started consolidating their military positions. In mid-April, the government in Sofia received reports of the mistreatment of ethnic Bulgarians living there. When it became known that the Greek navy helped move Serbian troops from Scutari to Macedonia, Tsar Ferdinand of Bulgaria started panicking. He thought that the invasion would come, and he ordered the removal of all works of art from Sofia. He also moved his personal residence, archives, and the seat of the foreign ministry.

The Greeks and Serbs bonded over more than just their issues with Bulgaria. Another common potential enemy was the new state of Albania. The London Conference gave Albania its independence, but this conflicted with Serbian and Greek interests in the region. The allies had to make sure Albania came into no contact with Bulgaria, as such an alliance would be a major threat to their goals. The Serbian prime minister told the ambassadors in London that Serbia would not allow Bulgaria to extend its territory in such a way that physical contact was made with Albania. He also urged the ambassadors to confine Bulgarian-controlled Macedonia to the right bank of the Vardar River. With this rhetoric, Prime Minister Nikola Pasic essentially admitted that Serbia had no intentions of following through with the March 1912 treaty. This was the point where the Bulgarians expected Russia to interfere and mediate the dispute, but the foreign ministry of Russia did nothing to resolve the issue between Serbia and Bulgaria. They chose to ignore their involvement in the issue of Macedonia, and with it, they condemned the Balkan League to collapse.

The Bulgarian government realized they couldn't do anything about their dispute with Serbia just yet. They first had to resolve their issue with Greece and dismantle the Serbian-Greek alliance. Only then would Bulgaria have a chance in the upcoming war against Serbia. Prime Minister Geshov tried to persuade the government to accept the Greeks' proposal of the exchange of territories, with which they would acquire most of southern Macedonia. In return, Bulgaria would abandon its claim on Thessaloniki. The Greeks welcomed a peaceful resolution with the Bulgarians, despite their commitment to their Serbian allies.

However, some members of the Bulgarian government wouldn't budge. Among them was Stoyan Danev, who was the most vocal advocate against arbitration. He was confident in Bulgaria's military power, and he was certain they would succeed in taking all of the territories they had claimed in the war. In May, new fighting erupted between the Greeks and Bulgarians stationed near the Struma River. The result was fifty dead soldiers on the Bulgarian side and the loss of their position at the Angista, a river in northern Greece.

Prime Minister Geshov also tried to reach a peaceful settlement with Serbia. If they managed to reason with Serbia, Bulgaria would only have to fight Greece. Geshov was confident this was a more reasonable path since the Bulgarian army was larger and better equipped than the Greeks. Also, Greece didn't have the support of any of the Great Powers and, therefore, was an easier target. The Bulgarians already thought of Macedonia as their territory, and in April of 1913, they formally asked Russia to arbitrate in the dispute under the terms set in the March 1912 treaty. Even though Russia played a role in giving Silesia to Romania, many Bulgarians continued to believe in the old friendship between their country and the Russian Empire. For them, it was impossible to imagine how Russia would liberate territory from the Ottomans just to give it to Serbia. The Russian foreign ministry again attempted to avoid the arbitration by simply ignoring the Bulgarians' formal request. In reality, the Russians wanted to remain in good relations with both Serbia and Bulgaria, and they knew that choosing a side would cost them one of their allies in the Balkans.

The Greek-Serbian alliance was finally formalized on May 5th, 1913. Greek state officials were aware of the upcoming war and their relative weakness compared to Bulgaria. They needed the Serbian Army if they had any hopes of winning the war, let alone preserving their conquered territories. The agreement between Serbia and Greece called for a common border in northern Macedonia, west of the Vardar River. If the new border wasn't accepted by Bulgaria, Serbia and Greece also agreed to provide each other with political and military support against their common enemy. This agreement, which essentially divided Macedonia between Greece and Serbia, was formally signed on May 14th, but the formal alliance wasn't signed until June 1st, 1913, a day after the London Ambassador Conference concluded. The treaty also divided Albania under Serbia's and Greece's spheres of influence. The Serbian government was aware this would antagonize Austria-Hungary, but a conflict with the Habsburg Empire was only a matter of time. The Austrians aspired to rid Europe of Serbia as a sovereign state because they proved to be a stubborn and dangerous neighbor.

By the end of April, both Serbia and Greece approached Romania, seeking an alliance. Romania shared interests with the Serbs and Greeks against Bulgaria, but they were not confident how Russia would react. They didn't want to antagonize their northern neighbor by attacking Bulgaria. The Greeks and Serbians also approached the Ottomans; however, no agreement emerged between these countries, although all parties hoped to gain something out of the ensuing war. The Montenegrins felt obliged to help their Serbian brethren, especially after the help they received at Scutari, and they devoted their army to the Greek-Serbian cause. However, they also secretly hoped they would acquire the Sanjak of Novi Pazar for themselves. On May 26th, the Serbian officials demanded the revision of the March 1912 treaty, but the Bulgarians refused.

The Conclusion of the First Balkan War

Bulgaria wanted to end the peace talks at the London Conference as soon as possible so they could move their army, which was stationed in Thrace, to Macedonia. Although the fronts at Gallipoli and Chataldja against the Ottomans were still open, the Bulgarians wanted to pursue their Macedonian interests rather than have their army trapped in Thrace. After all, Macedonia had always been their primary goal. But the Serbs and Greeks delayed signing the peace treaty because they needed to buy some time so they could consolidate their positions in Macedonia. However, the Great Powers pressured the parties involved to sign the treaty, and the Treaty of London was concluded on May 30th, 1913, bringing the formal end to the First Balkan War.

The Ottomans were forced by the Treaty of London to cede all the lands east of the line drawn between the Aegean port of Enez and the Black Sea port of Midia (today in Romania). With this line, the Ottoman Empire lost the control of both Adrianople and Lozengrad, and the only defense they could mount in the future would be at Chataldja, which would never provide Constantinople with sufficient protection. The Ottomans also had to cede the Aegean Islands to the Greeks, including Crete. The only islands they could retain were Imbros and Tenedos. They needed these islands to defend the Bosporus if the need arose.

The Great Powers took it upon themselves to draw the borders of the newly independent state of Albania, which proved to be the greatest problem of the peace conference. The recognition of Albania was a triumph for Austria-Hungary because the existence of the new state, which would be under the Habsburg sphere of influence, guaranteed that Austrian interests were met in the Balkans. Russia still had Bulgaria as its greatest Balkan ally, but that was about to change. Regardless, the Great Powers failed to include all of the Albanian population within the state's borders. This would prove to be a point of strife between Albania and its neighbors in the future. Kosovo was left out, and even Austria-Hungary, Albania's greatest advocate and ally, refused to include this province in the new state. The Albanian borders were finally concluded in August 1913.

The distribution of the European parts of the Ottoman Empire, except Albania, was left to be decided by the Balkan states. But this would only be resolved by a conflict between Bulgaria, Serbia, and Greece. Bulgaria did gain one advantage with the conclusion of the Treaty of London. The war with the Ottoman Empire was officially over, and they were now able to move their Thracian forces to confront the established Serbian and Greek presence in Macedonia.

Prime Minister Geshov resigned by the time the Treaty of London was signed. But before leaving office, Geshov met with Serbian Prime Minister Nikola Pasic on June 1ˢᵗ. They tried one last time to resolve the issue of Macedonia by diplomacy, but the meeting brought no resolution to the problem. War remained the only solution.

The Provocation

Stoyan Danev assumed the office of Bulgaria's prime minister on June 15ᵗʰ, 1913. He still hoped he could compel Serbia to accept the treaty from March 1912, and he still relied on Russia as an arbitrator. Danev trusted Russia, and he saw their stalling as bureaucratic lethargy. However, it wasn't that; Russia had yet to make up its mind. It didn't want to lose either of its Balkan allies, but the Russian tsar was afraid that Bulgaria would conquer Serbia. That would benefit Austria-Hungary, as Russia would lose its chance to establish a power base in the Balkans. Russian Foreign Minister Sergei Sazonov was also annoyed by Danev's attitude. In addition, he was still bothered by the claims the Bulgarians had laid on Constantinople during the First Balkan War.

Russia wasn't the only problem Bulgaria had to deal with. Another problem came from within its army. The soldiers were mostly peasants, and they have been fighting since 1912. They didn't want another war. They only wanted to go to their homes and live peacefully. This might explain why the Bulgarian army lacked morale and willingness during the inter-allied war.

The officers of the Bulgarian army were aware of the discontent that grew among their soldiers, and they urged the government to either disperse the troops and send them home or to start the war and send them to fight. After all, an idle army can be dangerous. But the Bulgarian military leaders predicted a victory against the Serbs and Greeks. Even though they lost many people during the war against the Ottomans, the Bulgarian army was still strong, and its officers didn't lack confidence. To urge the Russians to decide on mediating the Macedonia issue, Danev announced on June 24th that he expected an answer in seven days. Sazonov finally agreed to meet with the Serbian and Bulgarian representatives. Nikola Pasic and Stoyan Danev agreed to meet in St. Petersburg, where Russia would finally start the arbitration process.

The Bulgarian government could not have imagined that the Russians would abandon them. That was simply impossible, as they couldn't understand why Russia would help them fight off the Ottomans, only to abandon them for a lesser ally such as Serbia. Danev was aware Russia needed Bulgaria on its side because of its proximity to Constantinople and Bosporus. Serbia was far from these Russian points of interest, and the only thing it could offer was deepening the hostilities with Austria-Hungary. Danev understood that if Russia refused to deal with the Serbian-Bulgarian dispute, they would lean on the Serbian side by default. This might even push Romania to join Serbia and bring about a Serbian victory in the pending war.

So, Danev chose to rely on Bulgaria's friendly past with Russia. In the Russo-Turkish War (1877/78), the Russians helped free Bulgaria of Ottoman rule. In 1902, they signed a military convention, which was renewed in 1909 and 1911. Russia also stepped in to guarantee the March 1912 treaty and provided Bulgaria with substantial funds during the First Balkan War. Finally, many Bulgarian intellectuals had been educated in Russia, and upon their return to Bulgaria, they continued to advocate pro-Russian sentiment among the people.

The situation exploded even before the representatives of Serbia and Bulgaria departed for St. Petersburg. Since both Serbian and Bulgarian troops assumed their positions in Macedonia, they took the opportunity to provoke each other and engage in sniper attacks and occasional raids. On the night of June 29th, General Savov gained permission from Tsar Ferdinand to openly attack and try to take over the Serbian position in Macedonia. The Bulgarian army that was facing the Greek troops received a similar order. Tsar Ferdinand approved these actions because he feared Macedonian organizations within Bulgaria would launch an attempt on his life. But it was Savov who persuaded the tsar to approve the attack, as he was afraid many of his soldiers would desert even before the fighting started. That's how low morale in the Bulgarian army was. Although the peasants were still patriotic, they had little drive left to push them into the battle. The government in Sofia refused to recognize the order to attack. Danev later claimed he was not aware of the intentions of Tsar Ferdinand and General Savov. On the other hand, Danev made many provocative statements when addressing the population, which contributed to the rising tension.

The Bulgarian 2nd and 4th Armies were stationed in Macedonia. The rest of the army was still moving to its positions from Thrace. Danev tried to prevent the fighting by sending peaceful messages to Belgrade and Athens. He insisted Bulgaria still intended to meet Serbia in St. Petersburg and try to resolve the dispute by diplomacy. However, neither Greece nor Serbia responded. They didn't trust the Bulgarian government because they were aware of Danev's warmongering speeches to the people. After all, by allowing the Bulgarians to make the first move, the Serbian-Greek allies had an opportunity to present themselves as the victims of the ensuing conflict. This would also give them an advantage in the future resolution of Macedonia.

Chapter 8 – The War of the Allies: The Second Balkan War

*Bulgarian soldiers during the Second Balkan War as depicted in a
painting named* Na Nozh *by Yaroslav Veshin*
*https://commons.wikimedia.org/wiki/File:Yaroslav_Veshin_-
_Na_nozh.jpg*

When Bulgaria launched its attack on the Serbian and Greek forces on the night of June 29th, 1913, the hostilities that had been escalating between the allies during the First Balkan War finally culminated. All of the members of the Balkan League saw war as the only means by which the matter could be resolved. All three states were fighting over the control of Macedonia, and each one of them had a historical or cultural claim to it. But for the Greeks and Serbs, the fight meant so much more because Great Bulgaria (with Macedonia) would overpower them and become the dominant state in the region. Serbia and Greece needed to split Macedonia between themselves to balance power in the Balkans. Serbia would gain its northern part, including Skopje, while Greece would gain control over its southern part, together with Thessaloniki. But once the fighting began, Romania jumped in and tried to seize the opportunity to take over control of southern Dobruja. The Romanians were not the only ones who tried to gain something from the inter-allied war, as the Ottoman Empire attacked Bulgaria so it could retrieve control over Adrianople.

Preparations for the War

During the First Balkan War, the Serbian and Greek armies had few casualties because they faced weak Ottoman forces stationed in Europe that were cut off from their capital in Constantinople. Because of this, they had more numerous forces than Bulgaria, especially because they faced their enemy together. Aside from that, Serbia and Greece fought the First Balkan War for a shorter period of time than Bulgaria. Serbia's fight was over once they took over Bitola, and the Greeks besieged Ioannina until March 1913. And while they waited for their Bulgarian allies to finish their fighting, they used that time to strengthen their positions in Macedonia. The Bulgarian forces were exhausted and had been reduced n number by all the fighting in Thrace. They had no time to rest before they were ordered to march to Macedonia and attack their ex-allies.

However, Bulgaria had one advantage over the Serbian and Greek armies, as all of the internal communication and supply lines were under their control. Serbia and Greece had to coordinate their communication and supply lines because they were two separate countries, were divided over the disputed land of Macedonia, and spoke two very different languages. This made the Serbians and Greeks operate independently. Even though they communicated with each other, the command was divided. The Bulgarians were also united because they felt that their allies had betrayed them by occupying a territory that should belong to them. However, not all Bulgarians felt the same. Some of the soldiers weren't as enthusiastic as their officers. Some of them were tired of fighting and simply wanted to go home and continue their peaceful lives.

When the war started, the Bulgarians were in command of five armies, which were positioned along the line from the Danube River all the way to the Aegean Sea. This was a front over 300 miles (482 kilometers) long. Over 360,000 men fought as Bulgarian soldiers. The army was supplemented by young men brought from newly conquered regions in Thrace. General Vasil Kutinchev commanded the 1st Army, and they were stationed from Vidin to Brestovitsa. The 3rd Army was stationed north of Sofia, and it was commanded by General Radko Dimitriev. The 5th Army was newly organized under the command of General Stefan Toshev, and they were stationed in the far west of Bulgaria, around Radomir and Kyustendil. The 4th Army was led by General Stiliyan Kovachev, and their position was on the Zlatovska River. The 2nd Army, commanded by General Nikola Ivanov, was facing Greece. Their position was on the line between Kavala and Doiran Lake near Thessaloniki. There was also a small detachment of the Bulgarian army in Thessaloniki. The cavalry division proved less useful against the Ottomans, and in an attempt to avoid unnecessary losses, their new role in the Second Balkan War was only to protect the Bulgarian army's right flank. Therefore, they were stationed north of the 1st Army, close to the Danube River.

The Serbian Army was under the command of Voivode Radomir Putnik, and it numbered around 300,000 men. Around forty-eight thousand Serbian soldiers were not counted in this army since they were stationed along the newly settled border with Albania and didn't fight the Bulgarians. The army was divided into four groups. Crown Prince Alexander commanded the 1ˢᵗ Army, which was stationed just northeast of Skopje. General Bozidar Jankovic commanded the 3ʳᵈ Army, which was also stationed in Macedonia near Veles. The central group of the Serbian force was the 2ⁿᵈ Army, under the command of General Stepa Stepanovic. He fought together with the Bulgarians near Adrianople during the First Balkan War. Now, he was facing them at Pirot, a town in southeastern Serbia. The Timok Brigade was stationed at the Danube River to the east of Serbia, where the border with Bulgaria started. This army was under the command of Colonel Vukoman Aračić.

The Serbs were joined by 12,800 Montenegrins, who made up the Decani Brigade. Initially, they were attached to different parts of the Serbian Army, but after the Battle of Bregalnica, they were all attached to the 3ʳᵈ Army.

The Greek army was now under the command of King Constantine, who ascended the Greek throne after his father's assassination. He commanded nine divisions and a cavalry unit of around 121,000 men in total. They were all stationed north of Thessaloniki and faced the Bulgarian 2ⁿᵈ Army. Two separate divisions remained stationed in Epirus so Greece could enforce its claim of this region.

The Serbs and Greeks signed a military convention on June 1ˢᵗ in Thessaloniki. During this convention, they foresaw three possible plans of action. The first one was that the Greeks would come to help the Serbian offensive against the Bulgarians if the enemy forces were to be concentrated against Serbs. The second one predicted that the Bulgarian army would concentrate against Greece, in which case the Serbian Army would come to help their ally mount an offensive. The third plan was a general offensive against Bulgaria if the enemy split its forces to face the Serbs and Greeks at the same time. When it became obvious that the Bulgarians decided to face the Serbs in Macedonia, it was clear that the Bulgarians would act first and launch an attack. In that case, the Serbian Army had to mount a defense, but they also planned to push the Bulgarian army back and pursue them beyond Macedonia.

The Bulgarian army planned an overall attack, using all five armies it had at its disposal. They were going to simultaneously attack both the Serbs and Greeks. They were worried for their capital, Sofia, which was dangerously close to the Serbian border. To avoid fighting near the capital, they had to act first and launch an attack. But the rapid movement of the Bulgarian army was prevented by the hostile mountainous area of western Bulgaria and eastern Serbia and Macedonia. It was impossible to organize a linear movement of the whole army, as roads were few and soldiers often needed to disperse to conform to the mountains and hills in the region. The plan was that the 1ˢᵗ Army would enter the Serbian border near Knjazevac and then continue to Pirot. The 3ʳᵈ Army would go directly to Pirot, where it would meet the 1ˢᵗ Army. The 5ᵗʰ Army would be used to reinforce the flanks of the whole Bulgarian army and anchor it to the battlefield. The 4ᵗʰ Army was to attack Shtip in northern Macedonia, and the 2ⁿᵈ Army would march to southern Macedonia toward Gevgeli and Thessaloniki. This was the official plan of the Bulgarian high command, but it was never implemented.

The Battle of Bregalnica

The most important position from which Macedonia could be conquered was occupied by the Bulgarian 4ᵗʰ Army. The city of Shtip was at the center of this army, which spread around it in the shape of a bow. But this also meant that its flanks were left vulnerable to counterattacks. The first attack came on the night of June 29ᵗʰ when the Bulgarian 4ᵗʰ Army attacked the Serbian positions of its 1ˢᵗ and 3ʳᵈ Armies. Although the initial fighting occurred around the Zlatovska

River, the battle was named after the Bregalnica River, along which the Bulgarian army had to retreat. The Bulgarian army crossed the Zlatovska River and advanced against the Serbian flanks. After some heavy fighting, the left flank of the Bulgarian 4th Army managed to take the position at Udovo, near the Vardar River. But the center of the Bulgarian army didn't make any progress.

The government in Sofia failed to react to the situation on the battlefield due to confusion in the chain of command. Danev issued an order to Savov on July 1st to stop the fighting. But on the same day, Tsar Ferdinand ordered him to continue the battle as planned. When Savov failed to acknowledge the tsar's order, Ferdinand fired him. General Dimitriev, the commander of the 3rd Army, took his place. Dimitriev was a Russophile, and with his appointment, the Bulgarians hoped they would please St. Petersburg and instigate the Russians into intervening. However, all of these halts and changes of command halted the action on the battlefield, completely paralyzing the Bulgarian forces. Even though the 13th and the 7th Rila Divisions had the Serbs pinned down, they received an order to retreat to their original positions. The retreat was dangerous, though, as the Serbian forces were close, and the Bulgarians lost many soldiers during this unnecessary retreat.

This hiatus in the Bulgarian attack lasted for three days, and it was enough for the Serbs and Greeks to recover from the initial losses. They never stopped fighting, and they continued to fire on the Bulgarians even while they were retreating. Some Bulgarian officers tried to reason with the Greek and Serbian commanders, persuading them that the initial attack was a mistake. But it was to no avail, and the Serbs mounted their offensive on July 1st. The Serbian Army was pinned down by the first blow of the Bulgarian attack, and when General Jankovic requested permission to retreat, Voivode Putnik refused. Instead, he ordered a counterattack between Shtip and Kocani which succeeded in pushing the Bulgarian right flank back toward the Bregalnica River.

The lack of order among the ranks of the Bulgarian 5th Army contributed to the Serbian success. General Toshev of the 5th Army requested permission from the Bulgarian government to move his troops to Macedonia, but confirmation never came. Instead, they were ordered to attack the Serbian forces, and the order was later canceled after the soldiers had already engaged the enemy. Such muddled circumstances led to the failure of the 5th Army to achieve anything. By July 8th, the Bulgarians were retreating beyond the Bregalnica River, and their army sustained heavy losses. They counted around 20,000 casualties compared to Serbia's 16,600. Although the Battle of Bregalnica was a complete disaster, an even greater debacle occurred in Macedonia, where the Bulgarians fought the Greeks.

Bulgarian Defeat in Greece

The Bulgarian 2nd Army had difficulties since the fighting began on June 30th. This army had only thirty-six thousand men at its disposal, and twenty thousand of those were still untrained. Such as it was, the 2nd Army confronted almost the whole Greek army. Their orders came on June 26th, and the high command in Sofia wanted them to destroy all of the Greek forces in eastern Macedonia and continue to Thessaloniki. This was an impossible task, and it was beyond the capabilities of the Bulgarian army. Nevertheless, General Ivanov ordered the attack.

The Geeks responded to the initial attack with a counterattack. Just as the Bulgarians underestimated the Greek numbers stationed in Macedonia, the Greeks overestimated the Bulgarian numbers. They believed the enemy was attacking with at least eighty thousand men. The Greek army was divided into three groups: left, center, and right. They planned to resist the attack and push the Bulgarian troops back, but they would use their strong center and left flank to cut the Bulgarian retreat toward Strumica. They also hoped their left flank would meet the Serbian right flank, and the allies would drive the Bulgarians out of Macedonia together.

The Bulgarian 2nd Army was stretched along the 120-mile-long line, and the Greeks had no trouble putting pressure on both of its flanks. The Bulgarian positions in the Strymonian Gulf were constantly bombarded by Greek battleships in the Aegean Sea. The Greek infantry attacked the Bulgarian right flank and overpowered it without any problems. The 2nd Army had no other choice but to start retreating toward the left flank of the Bulgarian 4th Army, which was stationed near Strumica. At the time, the 4th Army was also in trouble, as it was experiencing heavy artillery fire, and as such, it was unable to offer support to the 2nd Army.

At Kilkis, north of Thessaloniki, the Bulgarians constructed heavy defenses. They dug trenches and made barriers equipped with guns. But after four days, they experienced such heavy attacks that they had to abandon this position. They tried to organize a counterattack that would bring them to their previous position, but they failed, even though the 2nd Army received support from the reserve forces from Sofia. As if the failure wasn't enough, their retreat uncovered the left flank of the Bulgarian 4th Army, forcing them to retreat as well.

The victory of the Greek forces over the Bulgarian 2nd Army was their greatest achievement during the Balkan Wars. It was also the worst defeat the Bulgarians experienced until then. More than 6,000 Bulgarian soldiers were taken prisoner, and 130 pieces of artillery were confiscated by the Greeks. But the Greek army's victory was costly, as it lost around 8,700 soldiers. With this defeat, Bulgaria lost its hope of retrieving the Aegean parts of Macedonia and Thessaloniki.

The Bulgarian unit stationed in the city of Thessaloniki was destroyed. The fighting between the Greek and Bulgarian garrisons in the city began on June 30th. The Bulgarian 3rd Battalion of the 14th Macedonian Regiment was completely isolated in the city, with no hope of escaping and meeting with the 2nd Army. They were outnumbered by the Greek 2nd Division and by the Cretan police stationed in Thessaloniki. Savov ordered the Bulgarian garrison in the city to retreat before the fighting started, but the government in Sofia dismissed his order. The Bulgarian soldiers needed to stay in the city to represent a symbolic occupation and Bulgaria's claim over Thessaloniki. The government decided it would rather sacrifice these soldiers than give up its claim on the city.

The Retreat

The Bulgarian government in Sofia finally settled the confusing situation with the chain of command in the Bulgarian army, and the attack resumed on July 4th. This time, the command was given to all of the armies at the same time, avoiding premature fighting and unorganized defenses.

However, the situation was irreversibly bad on the Macedonian front. The Serbian Army mounted such a vigorous counterattack that they pushed the whole Bulgarian 4th Army into a retreat. By July 7th, they retreated beyond the Bregalnica River, with the 2nd Army providing them with cover. Once the Bulgarian 4th Army was on the other bank of the river, it assumed a defensive position.

The Greeks defeated the right flank of the Bulgarian 2nd Army yet again. This time, the fighting occurred at Doiran Lake on July 7th, and the Bulgarians were forced to retreat to the northeast. The center of the Bulgarian 2nd Army strongly held up their position at Rupel Gorge, where they were able to control the Struma River route to the north. But by July 9th, the whole 2nd Army was pushed into a general retreat toward Gorna Dzhumaya (today's Blagoevgrad in Bulgaria). On the same day, the Greek armies entered Strumica, and three days later, they met the Serbian Army in Macedonia.

Although the center of the Bulgarian 5th Army made some progress against the Serbs, the retreat of the 2nd Army and the inability of the 4th Army to make an advance against their enemies caused the Bulgarians to fail. Even the previously successful 5th Army started having difficulties, and it started retreating on July 6th. This army would remain on the Bulgarian border until the end of the war. There, the

Bulgarians mounted a defense and prevented the Serbian and Greek armies from approaching Sofia. On two separate occasions, the Serbian Army attempted to break through these border defenses, but the Serbs were exhausted from the Battle of Bregalnica, so they were unable to advance. The front on the Bulgarian border would remain static until the end of the Second Balkan War.

The Bulgarian 3rd Army was divided into two groups, which approached Pirot and had the task to continue to Niš to cut the railroad that connected Serbian cities with Skopje. This would bring the communication and supply lines of the enemy armies to a halt. When the Bulgarians approached Pirot, Voivode Putnik of Serbia reorganized his armies and brought additional units from the south to defend Pirot. Although he saved the city, the movement of the armies prolonged the war. If the Serbian troops had remained in the south, they would have eventually been able to completely overwhelm the Bulgarian 2nd and 4th Armies and push into Bulgarian territory. This would have effectively ended the war. However, the 3rd Army was pushed back toward the Bulgarian border, where it assumed a defensive position. Sofia was only thirty miles southeast of Pirot, which was too close for the Bulgarian government to feel comfortable.

The Bulgarian 1st Army started its offensive on July 4th near the Serbian town of Knjazevac. There, they fought hard and broke the Serbian defense, then started southward toward Pirot. However, on July 8th, they received an order to retreat to the Bulgarian border. Though they were successful, the other armies were in such bad shape that the 1st Army had to be used to reinforce the borderline defensive positions. On its way home, the 1st Army was caught in a ravine where the Serbian forces had their artillery stationed. The Bulgarians were trapped, and the Serbs started firing at them, shooting over five thousand soldiers. The remainder of the Bulgarian 1st Army reached its destination only to be commanded to move to the south, where it was believed they would be of better use. But the movement of this army left northwestern Bulgaria exposed to an attack from Serbia and Romania.

By the time of high summer, both the Serbian and Bulgarian armies found themselves exhausted. The soldiers were unwilling to fight, and they would often achieve an informal truce with the enemy while their ranking officers would not do anything to punish them. On both the Serbian and Bulgarian sides, the soldiers would simply refuse to fight, though they continued to hold their positions. Even the officers were reluctant to order attacks, as they didn't want to unnecessarily sacrifice their soldiers when it was clear they would not make any significant advance.

All of the fronts eventually came to a halt. The allied Serbian and Greek forces couldn't break the Bulgarian border defenses, and the Bulgarians took the time to reorganize their army and improve their conditions. But just as they were stabilizing the front, two unexpected problems occurred that threatened to undermine all of the efforts the Bulgarians had made. One was Romania, which was, up until then, carefully observing the course of events. The second problem was the Ottoman Empire, which was eager to retrieve Adrianople, a strategically important city that offered an additional defense to their capital of Constantinople.

Romania Intervenes

Romania had remained neutral, although both Serbia and Greece approached it with offers of an alliance. But since Romania had aspirations to acquire southern Dobruja, it took the opportunity to attack Bulgaria once it saw the chances of a victory would be high. The mobilization of the Romanian army started on July 5th, though the war would only be declared on July 10th. Romania had a strong army of 94,170 regular men and 6,149 officers, and with massive mobilization, this army could easily grow to 417,720 men. They were well equipped and had 140 field batteries and 3 mountain batteries. This was the largest of all the Balkan armies, and if it was used properly, it could be a decisive factor in the Balkan Wars. However, the Romanians chose to remain neutral, as their army had not seen international action since 1878. With Romania joining the war, whatever little hopes the Bulgarians had of succeeding in their efforts against Greece and Serbia vanished.

When Romania declared war on Bulgaria, the Bucharest government made it known that they had no intention of destroying the Bulgarian army or thwarting its policies. Romania only wanted Dobruja, and the government sent around eighty thousand soldiers to occupy the territory between Tutrakan and Balchik. This was the territory Romania had been denied at St. Petersburg. The Romanian cavalry regiment occupied the port of Varna, fearing Bulgarian retaliation, but once it became apparent that there was no army stationed there, they retreated to Dobruja. To confirm the occupation of southern Dobruja, Crown Prince Ferdinand of Romania took his Danube Army of 250,000 men across the Bulgarian border on July 14th. They crossed the border at three points: Gigen, Oryahovo, and Nikopol.

The Bulgarian government decided not to respond to this threat from the north. After all, their forces were already busy fighting the Serbs and Greeks. When the Romanian army realized there was no resistance to its invasion, it divided into two groups and pushed forward. One group moved to the west, intending to occupy Mihailovgrad (present-day Montana, Bulgaria), while the other one moved to the south, intending to cross the Iskar River and reach Sofia.

The Romanian invasion of Dobruja was a decisive moment of the Second Balkan War. The front in the west was stable, and the Bulgarians were preparing a counteroffensive against the Serbs and Greeks. There was nothing they could do about Dobruja, and they were ready to sacrifice it to proceed with the war that would eventually bring Macedonia under their control. But when the Romanian army approached their capital, Bulgaria was in no position to prevent its occupation. On July 23rd, the Romanian army took the village of

Vrazhdebna, located just outside of Sofia (today one of the city's districts), and threatened to take over the capital. The Romanians even sent their aviators to take photos of the Bulgarian positions and its capital for reconnaissance purposes. They also installed fear in the citizens of Sofia by constantly maneuvering across the Bulgarian sky and dropping propaganda leaflets. However, they didn't fire a single shot. The Romanian army met the Serbian forces on July 25th at Belogradchik in northwestern Bulgaria, isolating the most important city of this region, Vidin, in the process. Together, the Serbian and Romanian armies were able to counter the Bulgarian 3rd Army.

Although the Romanians didn't fire a single shot, they did lose some soldiers when cholera appeared among its ranks. More than six thousand soldiers died of the disease, and once the surviving soldiers returned home, they spread cholera to the civilian population. These civilians were not victims of the war per se, but they were a price Romania had to pay to gain all of Dobruja.

Bulgaria would exercise its revenge on Romania during the First World War. With the help of the German and Austro-Hungarian armies, the Bulgarians would invade and defeat Romania, taking Dobruja back in the process.

The Ottoman Invasion

The collapse of the Balkan League and the start of the Second Balkan War alerted the Young Turks in the Ottoman Empire, who took the opportunity to regain what they had lost during the First Balkan War. Their main goal was Adrianople, and to take it, they moved their Chataldja and Gallipoli defenders on July 12th and crossed the new border set by the London Conference. The Ottoman army consisted of 250,000 men under the command of Ahmed Izzet Pasha.

In preparation for the war against Serbia and Greece, the Bulgarians pulled most of their army out of Thrace. Adrianople was guarded by a small garrison of only four thousand men, which was commanded by Major General Vulko Velchev. There were small forces dispersed throughout Eastern Thrace, but when faced with the renewed threat of their old enemy, the men retreated to the old border between Bulgaria and the Ottoman Empire. On July 19th, the Bulgarian garrison in Adrianople abandoned the city only to return the next day because the Ottomans hadn't arrived yet. However, on July 21st, they abandoned the city again, this time for good. The Ottoman army entered the city on July 23rd without firing a single shot.

But the Ottomans didn't stop with Adrianople. They continued into Bulgaria and advanced toward the town of Yambol. The Bulgarian civilians were terrified of their old enemy, and most of them ran to the mountains to save their lives. All the effort the Bulgarian army had achieved in Thrace just nine months prior was for nothing. The Turks were back, threatening Bulgaria's independence once again. Just like the Romanians, the Ottomans didn't have to fight to invade Bulgaria, and they suffered no casualties. However, they also had to deal with cholera among their ranks, and they lost around four thousand men.

Chapter 9 – War under the New Government

Greek soldiers passing through the Kresna Gorge
https://en.wikipedia.org/wiki/Battle_of_Kresna_Gorge#/media/File:Gr
eek_advance_Kresna_1913.jpg

Stojan Danev's pro-Russian government could not deal with the catastrophe on the battlefield, and he resigned on July 13th, 1913. Russia decided to stand aside and not meddle in the Balkan affairs, which shot down Bulgaria's hopes. Because of this, Danev's government lost the people's trust and came under direct attack by its political opponents. Four days later, a new government was formed, and it was made of politicians who despised Russia and turned to Germany and Austria-Hungary for help. The new government was headed by Vasil Radoslavov, and as soon as they took, they started searching for a diplomatic solution to the war.

Tsar Ferdinand used his ambassador in Italy to send a message to King Carol I of Romania on July 22nd. He managed to persuade the Romanian leader to halt his army and not proceed with the occupation of Sofia. Thus, the Bulgarian capital was saved.

The Great Powers, including Russia, started searching for ways to end the war as soon as possible. They appealed to Serbia and Romania to end the fighting. Serbian Prime Minister Nikola Pasic sent a message to Sofia, asking for a Bulgarian delegation to come to the city of Niš and take part in peace talks. Although the talks took place, they were inconclusive. The Serbian and Greek armies had the advantage, and they wanted to use the opportunity and occupy as much land as possible before the peace was concluded. However, they did come to one agreement: Bucharest would be the city in which the peace negotiations would continue. The Bulgarian delegation left Serbia on July 24th and headed straight to the Romanian capital.

Kalimantsi

Together with the new government, General Mihail Savov was brought back. He was given direct command over the 4th and 5th Armies to organize a defense against the Serbs. Southwest of the old border between Bulgaria and the Ottoman Empire, around the village of Kalimantsi near the Bregalnica River, the Bulgarian troops dug their defensive trenches and secured their position. They experienced the first attack of the Serbian 3rd Army and the Montenegrin division on July 18th.

The Serbian Army attempted to push the Bulgarians into a retreat by throwing hand grenades in their trenches, but the Bulgarians held firm. They even adopted a new tactic of providing weak fire so they could lure the Serbian troops to advance just so they could display their full artillery and massacre their enemy when they came too close. If they approached two hundred yards away from the trenches, the Bulgarian soldiers would jump out and use their bayonets to dispose of the enemy. The morale of the Bulgarian troops significantly increased because they were now defending their own country's borders from the invading armies.

The defense of the Bulgarian position was successful, and the Serbian Army reported 2,500 dead and more than 4,800 wounded. The Montenegrins had only 107 dead and 570 wounded. The fighting around Kalimantsi continued until the war ended, but the Serbs were never able to break their defenses and push the Bulgarian army into a retreat. If they had succeeded, they would have been able to reach the Bulgarian 2nd Army from the rear and probably destroy it. That would completely end the Bulgarian presence in Macedonia. The success of the 4th and 5th Armies under General Savov, as well as the defense of the 1st and 3rd Armies to the north, saved Bulgaria from the invading Serbian armies, which would have been capable of reaching Sofia.

Kresna Gorge

After the Bulgarian success at the defensive points against Serbia, the government was encouraged to order a counterattack against the Greeks. The Greek army pressed forward and successfully made the Bulgarians retreat. But by July 29th, the Bulgarian army gained the initiative and consolidated its defensive position again. But General Nikola Ivanov, the commander of the 2nd Army, lost his position and was replaced with General Savov, who mounted an excellent defense against the Serbs. Savov planned to lure the advancing Greek army to the area of Kresna Gorge near the Struma River, where the Bulgarian army would then launch a counterattack. There, the Struma River cuts through the Rhodope Mountains, creating a narrow pass. This was a perfect defensive position, especially since the Greeks had to exhaust their army to reach it due to the difficult terrain.

The Greek government was willing to accept an armistice at this point, and Prime Minister Venizelos only had to wait for the king's approval. However, King Constantine wanted a decisive victory on the battlefield, as it would put Greece in a much better negotiating position. The armistice would have to wait.

In the meantime, the Bulgarian high command decided to move the 1st Army from the northwestern fringes of Bulgaria to Macedonia and use it to reinforce the 2nd Army. By doing this, the Bulgarians were capable of preventing a Greek invasion. Then they would use the center and the right flank to launch a counterattack on the Greek positions. The plan was successful, and on July 29th, the Bulgarians managed to push the Greek army back to the valley of the Struma and Mesta Rivers. Then the Bulgarians sent their left flank down the Struma River valley and the right flank down the Mesta River valley to encircle the Greek army. The Greeks were unable to organize a proper defense because the rugged terrain prevented them from bringing their artillery.

This was the point in the Second Balkan War when the inability of the Serbian and Greek commanders to effectively coordinate their attacks became the most obstructive. When Greece asked their ally for help, they received no response. However, this was because the Serbs were in no position to offer help after the debacle at Kalimantsi, not because they didn't want to help. By July 30th, the Greeks faced the possibility of complete annihilation. King Constantine finally gave in and sent a telegram to Prime Minister Venizelos, who was already in Bucharest. He approved the armistice and urged his prime minister to end the hostilities as soon as possible.

King Constantine was in the field with his troops, and he was the prime example of royal military leadership. Nevertheless, his efforts to pursue the Bulgarians within their own country were unnecessary. The Greeks already occupied the parts of Macedonia they wanted to gain, so he needlessly risked his soldiers. But even before the Greek army found itself in this impossible situation at Kresna Gorge, the Bulgarian army received a ceasefire order.

With the Romanians so deep within their territory and with the Ottoman Empire penetrating their southeastern border, Prime Minister Radoslavov realized he needed to pursue diplomatic means to peace. If they were to attack the surrounded Greek army, the Bulgarians would gain the image of a villain, which would greatly diminish their position to negotiate peace terms. On July 31ˢᵗ, Bulgarian representatives in Bucharest agreed to a general armistice, saving the Greek army in the process. But even this success over their enemies was not enough to save the Bulgarian efforts. They had lost their claim over Macedonia, and the territory they gained in Thrace during the First Balkan War was lost to the Ottoman Empire.

Vidin

When the Bulgarian high command transferred the 1ˢᵗ Army to Macedonia to reinforce the 2ⁿᵈ Army's fight against Greece, the Serbs gained a chance to advance to northwestern Bulgaria. The fortified city of Vidin lay there, but it had very limited defenses. In total, only 5,730 Bulgarian soldiers were defending the city, and that included the local militia. Directly across the Danube, a detachment of the Romanian army concentrated around the town of Calafat. These two armies successfully surrounded Vidin, isolating it from the rest of Bulgaria. However, they were unable to take the city before the armistice was concluded. Had the war continued, Vidin would probably have been taken by the Serbian forces because of its isolation and poor defenses.

The Treaty of Bucharest

The peace delegations of Bulgaria, Serbia, and Greece met in Bucharest on July 30ᵗʰ. Montenegro also sent its representative, Prime Minister Janko Vukotic. Romania was the host, and the head of the peace talks was Romanian Prime Minister Titu Maiorescu. The Great

Powers also maintained their presence in the negotiations through their ambassadors in Bucharest. They refrained from dominating the assembly and chose to assert their influence from the background. The Ottoman Empire wanted to join the conference in Bucharest, but the Romanians rejected this, stating that the peace talks were organized mainly to settle the dispute between the Balkan allies. This meant that the Bulgarians would have to deal with the Ottomans without the help of the foreign powers. The Second Balkan War lasted for thirty-three days, and the warring parties agreed to a five-day armistice to conclude the peace.

The Bulgarian delegation in Bucharest was led by the new finance minister, Dimitar Tonchev. He replaced Prime Minister Radoslavov because he didn't want to accept a Bulgarian defeat. In addition, Radoslavov was also known for his very weak diplomatic skills. Tonchev devised a strategy by which he would divide the victorious coalition of Serbia, Montenegro, Greece, and Romania. However, the coalition acted as a unified front, and the Bulgarian representative was unable to shake them.

The Bulgarians reached their first settlement with Romania. Southern Dobruja was finally in Romanian hands. The Romanians also didn't want Serbia and Greece to grow too powerful. If they could keep the Greek-Serbian coalition weak, Romania would become the single most powerful state in the Balkans.

The settlement between Bulgaria and its former allies of the Balkan League was very difficult to achieve. Serbia laid claim on Macedonian territory to the Struma River valley, which meant Bulgaria would receive nothing. However, Russia and Austria-Hungary put pressure on Serbia to moderate its demands. Russia wanted to remain as a relevant force in Sofia, and Austria-Hungary wanted a small and weak Serbia. Prime Minister Nikola Pasic of Serbia was only willing to cede the town of Shtip.

Bulgaria had difficulties agreeing with Greece over who would take control of the Aegean port of Kavala. The Bulgarians had already lost Thessaloniki, and they needed at least one commercial port on the other side of the Rhodope Mountains. Kavala was a perfect choice because it was a rich tobacco-producing region. However, the Greeks refused to cede the port. The Greeks previously offered Kavala, Drama, and Serres in exchange for Thessaloniki, but the Bulgarians declined. Now that the Greeks were the victors, they didn't feel as if they owed anything to Bulgaria. Once again, Austria-Hungary and Russia paired up to support the Bulgarian claim of Kavala, but Germany and France took Greece's side. This demonstrated that even the Great Powers were not united when it came to the issues in the Balkans. The result was Bulgaria obtaining an undeveloped port at Dedeagach (now Alexandroupoli, Greece). It was their only Aegean outlet.

The Montenegrins had no territorial disputes with Bulgaria. They joined the war only to support Serbia so they could be awarded some of the territories in the Sanjak of Novi Pazar. They sent their delegation to Bucharest only to put pressure on Serbia to keep its promise. Although they failed to occupy this territory during the war, Serbia granted them control over it. The division of Sanjak between Serbia and Montenegro was confirmed in Belgrade on November 7th, 1913.

By August 8th, all the delegates in Bucharest concluded their work. The Treaty of Bucharest was signed on August 10th. Macedonia was divided into three parts, and this was the most significant achievement of the treaty. The Aegean regions of Macedonia were now under Greek control. Serbia gained the largest portion of Macedonia—the whole area of the Vardar watershed. This meant they also received the disputed zone that had been claimed by Bulgaria in the March 1912 treaty. The southwestern corner of the region, known as Pirin Macedonia, was given to Bulgaria.

Greece and Serbia considered the Treaty of Bucharest a great success, as it went beyond their expectations. They didn't only gain the territories they had wanted; they also weakened the position of Bulgaria in the Balkan Peninsula. Serbia was the strongest military power south of Danube, and it gained Russian patronage after the signing of the Treaty of Bucharest. Romania remained the strongest Balkan military power, and with its control of the whole Dobruja region, they prevented Bulgarian unity, further weakening Bulgaria's position in the Balkans. However, the peaceful Romanians refused to be considered a threat by their neighbors. They assumed the role of arbitrators of the whole Balkan region.

The Bucharest conference was a disaster for Bulgaria. Although they retained some of the territories they had gained during the First Balkan War, they lost the only goal for which they were fighting, Macedonia. The small portion they got was not enough to justify the army's sacrifices. Bulgaria fought two wars in a very short time, and its army was overly exhausted. However, they could not help but regard the Treaty of Bucharest as a temporary solution. They were determined to change the situation with or without the help of the Great Powers.

The Treaty of Constantinople

Since Romania refused to admit the Ottoman Empire at the Bucharest conference, the Bulgarians were forced to approach Constantinople and sue for peace. The Ottomans had already reoccupied most of Eastern Thrace, and they even penetrated the old Bulgarian border. None of the Great Powers showed any interest in supporting Bulgaria in its peace talks with the Ottomans, not even Russia, which considered Constantinople its natural inheritance. The peace talks in the capital of the Ottoman Empire began on September 6th, 1913. Among the Bulgarian representatives were General Savov; the ambassador to Constantinople, Andrey Toshev; and Bulgarian diplomat Grigor Nachovich. The Ottoman delegation consisted of foreign ministers Mehmed Talaat Bey, Mahmud Pasha, and Halil Bey.

The Bulgarians hoped they would be able to persuade the Ottomans to give back Lozengrad, but the Ottomans refused. In fact, the Turkish representatives stated that everything they took should be theirs. Everything the Bulgarians had achieved in Thrace during the First Balkan War went to the Ottomans. They lost Lozengrad, Lule Burgas, Bunarhisar, and Adrianople. All the blood the Bulgarians had spilled in the soil of Eastern Thrace was in vain. The only portion of land that they managed to retain was a small corner of Eastern Thrace that bordered the Black Sea.

However, the Bulgarian government would not accept this total defeat. They had to gain at least something from the Constantinople conference. So, Radoslavov sought to strengthen the relations between Bulgaria and the Ottoman Empire. The plan was to bind the Turks into an alliance that would help Bulgaria gain Macedonia when it renewed the war with Serbia and Greece. The Treaty of Constantinople was signed on September 30th, although the alliance wasn't achieved then. The negotiations continued throughout autumn, and a definitive agreement was never reached. Bulgaria and the Ottoman Empire would become allies only in 1915 when Bulgaria joined the Central Powers during World War I.

The Treaty of Constantinople was another debacle for the Bulgarians. Eastern Thrace was completely lost, but this loss was not as emotional as the one in Macedonia. After all, most of the population that inhabited Thrace was not Bulgarian. But for the Ottoman Empire, the Treaty of Constantinople was a great success. It served to lessen the bitterness of the First Balkan War and the loss of all of the Balkan territories that were once ruled by the Ottomans. Most importantly, the Ottomans regained Adrianople, which became their first European capital. This fortified city was an additional defense to Constantinople.

Both the Treaty of Bucharest and the Treaty of Constantinople didn't end the Balkan Wars. The fighting continued between Greece and the Ottoman Empire until the Treaty of Athens was signed on November 14th, 1913. This treaty concluded the conflict, but the question of the Aegean Islands was never resolved, and it would remain open until the Great Powers resolved it in July 1914. The relations between the Ottoman Empire and Greece continued to deteriorate, and war almost broke out in the spring of 1914. It finally erupted in 1922. Even today, Greece and Turkey struggle to normalize their relations.

The conflict between the Ottomans and Serbs ended with the signing of the Treaty of Constantinople on March 14th, 1914, although the two armies seldom met. Montenegro never officially signed a peace treaty with the Ottoman Empire. The Balkan Wars were officially over with this second treaty of Constantinople signed by the Ottoman Empire and Serbia. However, the whole region of the Balkan Peninsula would again rage in war just ten months later. Known at the time as the Great War, it would soon spread through Europe and then the whole world.

Conclusion

The Balkan Wars presented the nations inhabiting this region with a unique opportunity to establish a union. However, this opportunity was missed, and unity in the Balkan Peninsula was never achieved. If Bulgaria and Serbia kept to their agreement of 1912, they could have brought economic development to the whole region. The wasted lives and blood spilled in later wars could have been avoided. A unified Balkan Peninsula would have also been able to dissuade Austria-Hungary from its attempts to get rid of Serbia, something that would eventually lead to the outbreak of World War I.

This possible alliance failed for three main reasons. Bulgaria was reluctant to share Macedonia with its allies. It had unrealistic expectations of retaining the whole region, including Thessaloniki. The second reason was Austria-Hungary's and Italy's meddling, as both of them had interests in the Adriatic Sea. To thwart Greek and Serbian aspirations, they created an independent Albanian state, which would only contribute to the instability of the Balkan region. And finally, there was Russia's attitude or, better yet, the lack of it. Russia failed to pacify Serbia and Bulgaria, as it refused to arbitrate in the Macedonian dispute.

The Ottomans also had the chance to end the conflict early on, but they failed to exploit the fissures that existed among the Balkan League members. They concentrated on Bulgaria because of its proximity to Constantinople, and they failed to make arrangements with Serbia and Greece by ceding Kosovo and Macedonia. Instead, the Ottomans tried to defend all of their European possessions, and as a result, they lost them all.

At the end of the Balkan Wars, none of the participants were fully satisfied. The Bulgarians had experienced an enormous victory against the Ottoman Empire just to lose it all. Because they were greedy over Thessaloniki and Adrianople, they lost their main objective of Macedonia. In the end, they were unable to retain even Thessaloniki and Adrianople. And if that wasn't enough, the Bulgarians failed to achieve an agreement with Romania and also lost Dobruja. Bulgaria went from being the country with the most powerful army in the Balkans to the only country invaded on all of its fronts. The bitterness Bulgaria experienced with the loss of Macedonia led it to eventually join the Central Powers during World War I and the Axis Powers during World War II. These bad political decisions pushed Macedonia out of Bulgaria's reach forever.

Greece and Serbia achieved victories during both Balkan wars, but their armies were exhausted. They also suffered economic drawbacks, which would lead to foreign occupation during World War I. When Greece tried to reestablish its presence in Anatolia during 1921 and 1922, it only brought about the complete eradication of millennia-old Hellenic existence from this region and Eastern Thrace. The economically and military exhausted country had to deal with thousands of refugees.

Serbia, on the other hand, was the biggest winner of the Balkan Wars. It managed to expand its territory and population, and it achieved major victories against the Ottoman Empire and Bulgaria. Serbia gained prestige it had never enjoyed before, but the wars also brought it even bigger national aspirations. After the Balkan Wars,

Serbia turned its attention toward Bosnia, where the majority of the population was Serbian. Austria-Hungary felt threatened by Serbia even more, and just one year after the Treaty of Bucharest, it attempted to invade Serbia but failed. However, the third invasion in 1915 was successful, and Serbia would have to deal with foreign occupation. At the end of the world wars, Serbia emerged as a winner once again.

Montenegro gained lots of territory after the Balkan Wars, but its military failure proved that the Petrovic dynasty was unfit to rule the Serbian lands. Montenegro had to give up its dreams of ruling the Kingdom of Serbia as well as the Montenegrin state. Serbia became so powerful that it started drawing the population of Montenegro to Belgrade, and finally, Montenegro lost its independence in 1918. Many years later, in 2006, it would regain this independence peacefully.

The Young Turks were the only losers-turned-winners in the Balkan Wars, and they were the only ones who managed to achieve a complete national state. Their vision of Ottoman identity ultimately failed, but they managed to create Turkish nationalism. However, the Young Turks had to pay the price to achieve this. They had to suffer a defeat in the First World War, which brought about the end of the Ottoman Empire, and they also continued fighting over their Anatolian interests with Greece. It was followed by the Turkish War of Independence (1919–1923), and when it ended, the Republic of Turkey was established, with Mustafa Kemal Atatürk as its first president. Atatürk's efforts brought about reforms that modernized Turkey and turned it into one of the most democratic and secular states of the eastern world.

Here's another book by Captivating History that you might like

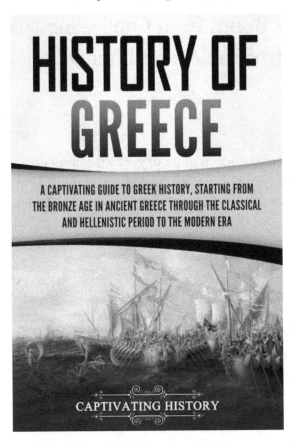

Free Bonus from Captivating History (Available for a Limited time)

Hi History Lovers!

Now you have a chance to join our exclusive history list so you can get your first history ebook for free as well as discounts and a potential to get more history books for free! Simply visit the link below to join.

Captivatinghistory.com/ebook

Also, make sure to follow us on Facebook, Twitter and Youtube by searching for Captivating History.

References

Buchanan, T., & Pettifer, J. (2015). *War in the Balkans: Conflict and Diplomacy before World War I*. I. B. Tauris & Company, Limited.

Fragistas, C. (1962). *The Balkan Wars: Their Meaning in the History of Greece*. Thessaloniki.

Geppert, D., Mulligan, W., & Rose, A. (2016). *The Wars before the Great War: Conflict and International Politics before the Outbreak of the First World War*. Cambridge: Cambridge University Press.

Geshov, I. E., & Mincoff, C. C. (1915). *The Balkan League*. London: J. Murray.

Glenny, M. (2018). *The Balkans: Nationalism, War, and the Great Powers, 1804-2012*. London: Granta.

Gooch, G. P., Temperley, H. W., & Penson, L. M. (1933). *The Balkan Wars*. London: His Majesty's Stationery Office.

Hall, R. C. (2010). *Balkan Breakthrough: The Battle of Dobro Pole 1918*. Bloomington: Indiana University Press.

Schurman, J. G. (2020). *The Balkan Wars*. S.l.: Duke Classics.